This book belongs to:

LEISURE ARTS, INC.
Little Rock, Arkansas

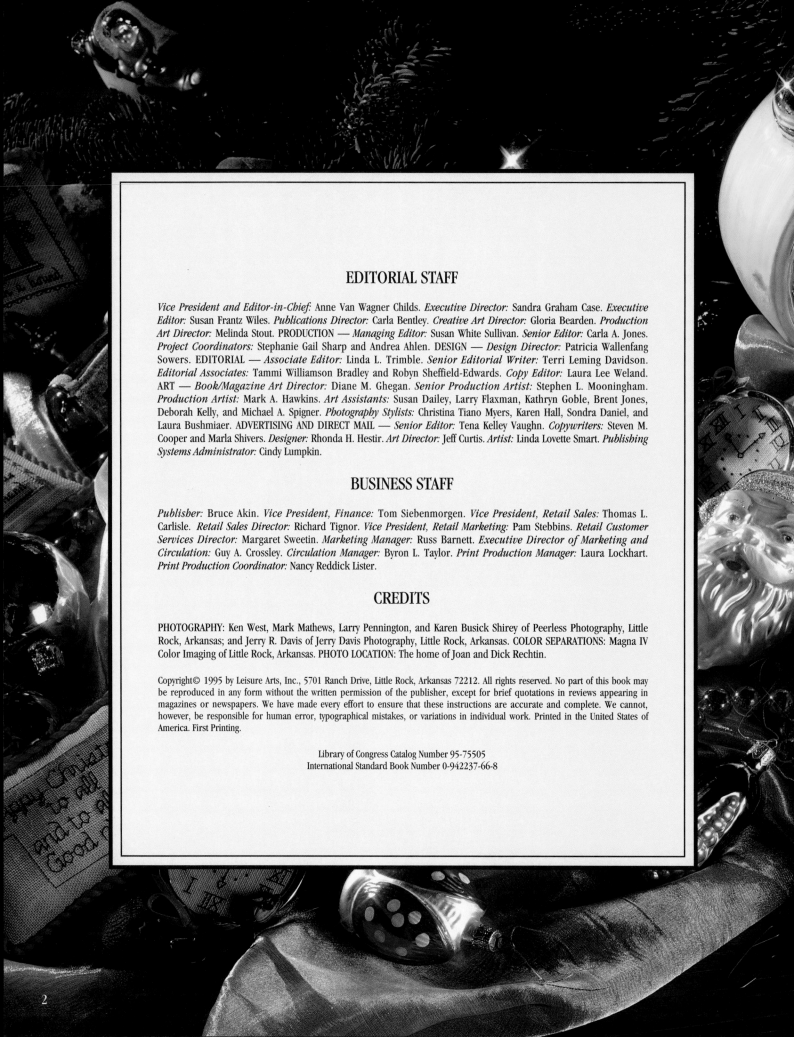

EDITORIAL STAFF

Vice President and Editor-in-Chief: Anne Van Wagner Childs. *Executive Director:* Sandra Graham Case. *Executive Editor:* Susan Frantz Wiles. *Publications Director:* Carla Bentley. *Creative Art Director:* Gloria Bearden. *Production Art Director:* Melinda Stout. PRODUCTION — *Managing Editor:* Susan White Sullivan. *Senior Editor:* Carla A. Jones. *Project Coordinators:* Stephanie Gail Sharp and Andrea Ahlen. DESIGN — *Design Director:* Patricia Wallenfang Sowers. EDITORIAL — *Associate Editor:* Linda L. Trimble. *Senior Editorial Writer:* Terri Leming Davidson. *Editorial Associates:* Tammi Williamson Bradley and Robyn Sheffield-Edwards. *Copy Editor:* Laura Lee Weland. ART — *Book/Magazine Art Director:* Diane M. Ghegan. *Senior Production Artist:* Stephen L. Mooningham. *Production Artist:* Mark A. Hawkins. *Art Assistants:* Susan Dailey, Larry Flaxman, Kathryn Goble, Brent Jones, Deborah Kelly, and Michael A. Spigner. *Photography Stylists:* Christina Tiano Myers, Karen Hall, Sondra Daniel, and Laura Bushmiaer. ADVERTISING AND DIRECT MAIL — *Senior Editor:* Tena Kelley Vaughn. *Copywriters:* Steven M. Cooper and Marla Shivers. *Designer:* Rhonda H. Hestir. *Art Director:* Jeff Curtis. *Artist:* Linda Lovette Smart. *Publishing Systems Administrator:* Cindy Lumpkin.

BUSINESS STAFF

Publisher: Bruce Akin. *Vice President, Finance:* Tom Siebenmorgen. *Vice President, Retail Sales:* Thomas L. Carlisle. *Retail Sales Director:* Richard Tignor. *Vice President, Retail Marketing:* Pam Stebbins. *Retail Customer Services Director:* Margaret Sweetin. *Marketing Manager:* Russ Barnett. *Executive Director of Marketing and Circulation:* Guy A. Crossley. *Circulation Manager:* Byron L. Taylor. *Print Production Manager:* Laura Lockhart. *Print Production Coordinator:* Nancy Reddick Lister.

CREDITS

PHOTOGRAPHY: Ken West, Mark Mathews, Larry Pennington, and Karen Busick Shirey of Peerless Photography, Little Rock, Arkansas; and Jerry R. Davis of Jerry Davis Photography, Little Rock, Arkansas. COLOR SEPARATIONS: Magna IV Color Imaging of Little Rock, Arkansas. PHOTO LOCATION: The home of Joan and Dick Rechtin.

Library of Congress Catalog Number 95-75505
International Standard Book Number 0-942237-66-8

INTRODUCTION

One of the most beloved symbols of the holiday season, the richly adorned Christmas tree that enthralls our hearts today is relatively new to the Yuletide celebration. Before the 1800's, festively laden firs were usually only seen in the quaint mountain burgs of Germany. There, the Christbaum (literally, "Christ-tree") was adorned with paper roses, apples, and communion wafers — all hallowed emblems of the holiday. This remained a mostly German custom until Prince Albert, Queen Victoria's royal consort, introduced the Christmas tree to England, and a legacy was born. The world was captivated by the gaiety of elaborate evergreens embellished with glacéed fruit, gilded leaves, and penny toys. Today, we couldn't imagine a Noel without the magic of the Christmas tree and its adornments! In this nostalgic volume, we've captured enchanting images from Victorian postcards, lithographs, and ornamental scraps to create truly timeless ornaments. You and your family will adore adding these cross-stitched heirlooms to your collection or using them to create a unique theme for the evergreen. May their charm evoke fond memories and add to your joy this season — and each Christmas to come.

TABLE OF CONTENTS

heartfelt messages

Proclaiming sentiments of the season, holly-trimmed ornaments bring tidings of love, hope, peace, and kindness to the celebration. The expressive tree-trims also make heartfelt holiday tokens to share with family and friends.

The spirit of Christmas is peace

The warmth of Christmas is kindness

heavenly host

As the news of Christ's birth spread across heaven and earth, multitudes of angels sounded their golden harps and lifted their voices in praise. From their pillowy clouds, they proclaimed God's glory with wishes of peace and harmony throughout the land.

Charts on pages 52 and 53

THE NIGHT BEFORE CHRISTMAS

Twas the night before Christmas, when all through the house Not a creature was stirring, not even a mouse; The stockings were hung by the chimney with care, In hopes that St. Nicholas soon would be there. The children were nestled all snug in their beds, While visions of sugar-plums danced through their heads; And mamma in her kerchief, and I in my cap Had just settled our brains for a long winter's nap, — When out on the lawn there arose such a clatter, I sprang from my bed to see what was the matter. Away to the window I flew like a flash, Tore open the shutters and threw up the sash. The moon, on the breast of the new-fallen snow, Gave the lustre of midday to objects below; When what to my wondering eyes should appear, But a miniature sleigh and eight tiny reindeer, With a little old driver, so lively and quick I knew in a moment it must be St. Nick. More rapid than eagles his coursers they came, And he whistled and shouted and called them by name: "Now, Dasher! now, Dancer! now, Prancer and Vixen! On, Comet! on, Cupid! on, Donder and Blitzen! To the top of the porch, to the top of the wall! Now, dash away, dash away, dash away all!" As dry leaves that before the wild hurricane fly, When they meet with an obstacle, mount to the sky, So, up to the house-top the coursers they flew, With the sleigh full of toys, — and St. Nicholas too. And then in a twinkling I heard on the roof The prancing and pawing of each little hoof. As I drew in my head, and was turning around, Down the chimney St. Nicholas came with a bound. He was dressed all in fur from his head to his foot, And his clothes were all tarnished with ashes and soot; A bundle of toys he had flung on his back, And he looked like a peddler just opening his pack. His eyes how they twinkled! his dimples how merry! His cheeks were like roses, his nose like a cherry; His droll little mouth was drawn up like a bow, And the beard on his chin was as white as the snow. The stump of a pipe he held tight in his teeth, And the smoke it encircled his head like a wreath. He had a broad face, and a little round belly That shook, when he laughed, like a bowl full of jelly. He was chubby and plump, — a right jolly old elf — And I laughed, when I saw him, in spite of myself. A wink of his eye and a twist of his head Soon gave me to know I had nothing to dread. He spoke not a word, but went straight to his work, And filled all the stockings; then turned with a jerk, And laying his finger aside of his nose, And giving a nod, up the chimney he rose. He sprang to his sleigh, to his team gave a whistle, And away they all flew like the down of a thistle; But I heard him exclaim, ere he drove out of sight: "Happy Christmas to all, and to all a good-night!"

— CLEMENT CLARKE MOORE

Charts on pages 54 and 55

The tale of Santa's magical journey is immortalized in
the classic poem penned by Clement Clarke Moore.
Illustrated with whimsical scenes, these timeless verses
will raise hopes that St. Nick soon will appear.

Down the chimney St. Nicholas came with a bound

In wink of his eye and a twist of his head

And filled all the stockings then turned with a jerk

Happy Christmas to all and to all a Good night!

Charts on pages 54-57

13

CHRISTMAS PERENNIALS

Crowned in holiday splendor, vibrant winter blossoms and berries provide a joyous contrast to the frosty landscape of the season. These bountiful gifts from nature — white chrysanthemum, poinsettia, holly, Christmas cactus, and mistletoe — have long been favorite Yuletide adornments.

Charts on page 58

15

QUILTS OF THE BIBLE

Quilters of yesteryear bestowed upon us a beautiful legacy for the Yuletide celebration. Their hand-pieced expressions of faith recounted the Christmas story through patterns such as Carpenter's Wheel, Star of the Magi, Shepherd's Crossing, Road to Jerusalem, and Bethlehem Star. Viewing these rich mosaics today, we can still imagine each wondrous tale unfolding.

Charts on pages 60 and 61

good cheer elves

Perched among the branches of their woodland home, these merry elves are eager for an evening of frolicking fun. Good-luck toadstools and twigs for the fire are gathered from the forest as the tiny woodsmen prepare to work their elfin magic. According to medieval lore, if you leave them a bowl of rice pudding to enjoy, they'll grant you good cheer throughout the year!

GOOD CHEER
TO YOU AND
ALL THOSE NEAR
and DEAR TO YOU

Chart on page 62

Charts on pages 62 and 63

Charts on pages 62 and 63

21

YOUNG AT HEART

As we share in the revelry of the holiday, we pause to reflect on the simple pleasures of our childhood. Precious memories of innocent games and handcrafted treasures keep us young at heart, knowing that we'll relive those cherished times with our children. The joy a newborn babe brings to a home is wonderfully magnified at Christmastide. Handcrafted mementos preserve those special memories of a child's first holiday season.

Charts on page 65

Hang up the baby's
stocking,
Be sure you don't
forget,
The little dimpled
Darling
Has ne'er seen
Christmas yet!

Chart on page 64

23

SCHOOLGIRL EMBROIDERIES

In pioneer homes, families trimmed their freshly cut Christmas trees with ornaments as primitive as their lifestyle. Scraps of fabric, empty thread spools, and stray buttons often provided simple yet charming accents. Perhaps most touching of all were handcrafted ornaments bearing the careful, deliberate stitches and childish sentiments of schoolgirls.

Chart on page 66

Charts on pages 66 and 67

paper doll teddy

Memories of childhood Christmases await with these nostalgic decorations. Long ago, a paper doll with a quick-change wardrobe was sure to be found among a youngster's playthings. With this charming teddy bear doll and Santa Claus clothing, we've recaptured the magic of those imaginative hours.

Chart on page 68

Charts on pages 68 and 69

PRETTY SAMPLING

Elegant silhouettes and tiny samplers offer charming tributes to Yuletide traditions. Depicting holiday scenes or symbols, these ornaments are simple reminders of the peaceful blessings bestowed upon the earth.

Charts on page 74

Chart on page 70

Before becoming the crimson-clad elf we know today, Saint Nicholas was often shown robed in snowy white or tranquil blue. But always he has been the generous gentleman who delivers his abundant gifts around the world while wintry villages slumber.

Charts on pages 72 and 73

VICTORIAN ANGELS

Celestial messengers who heralded the good news of the
Christ Child's birth, angels are beloved members of the Christmas
pageant. Crowned with golden stars and halos of greenery, our
sweet-faced cherubs recall the joy of the first Noel.

Chart on page 75

Charts on pages 75-77

33

FROSTY FRIENDS

With the first grand snowfall of winter, we share our children's delight in rolling handfuls of flakes into frosty new friends. Our imaginations create a whimsical personality for each snowman using old caps, scarves, and brooms. Whether peering through an icy windowpane or adorning tiny mittens, these chilly chaps will bring that wintry fun indoors.

Chart on page 78

Charts on page 79

RADIANT NATIVITY

Scattered among the boughs of the Christmas tree or assembled in a humble manger scene, beaded Nativity figures offer an endearing portrait of the Holy Birth. Heavenly angels, adoring shepherds, and gift-bearing Magi celebrate the wondrous moment as Mary and Joseph watch over the peaceful babe.

The glory of the Lord shown round about them. Luke 2:9

Chart on page 80

Charts on pages 80-83

And this shall be a sign unto you, ye shall find the babe wrapped in swaddling clothes, lying in a manger. And suddenly there was with the angel a multitude of heavenly host praising God, and saying, Glory to God in the highest, and on earth peace, goodwill toward men.

— LUKE 2:12-14

Charts on pages 80-83

MERRY MINI STOCKINGS

Enhanced with elegant touches, these stockings are tiny treasure troves for sweet surprises. The beaded collection shimmers with Victorian-style patterns, and scalloped lace trims our visions of Santa. His flowing white beard creates swirls of softness on the stockings.

Charts on page 85

Charts on page 84

NOAH'S ANIMALS

During the holidays, our hearts and minds are filled with thoughts of the Bible's miracles. Not only do we celebrate the story of Christ's holy birth, but we also reflect on other favorite passages, such as the account of Noah and the Great Flood. In years past, when only Biblical playthings were permitted on the Lord's Day, Noah's Ark toys were often favorite choices.

Charts on pages 86 and 87

SANTA'S TOYLAND

There's nothing Santa
more enjoys
Than making toys for
girls and boys.
And in his way he's
wondrous wise
For he knows just
what'll please
your eyes.

— AN OLD-TIME VERSE

Charts on pages 88-89

Charts on pages 90 and 91

*N*estled high atop the world at the snow-capped North Pole, Santa's toyshop hums with activity all year. While the jolly old gent checks his list and makes the final inspections, his trusty elves test cuddly dolls and teddies for their huggability and tin drums for their perfect beat. Even today, the happy toy-makers still believe that the best playthings are those powered by love.

Chart on page 90

ENDEARING SNOW BABIES

A *playful snowball fight, a few teetering strides on new skates, a cushioned tumble in new-fallen drifts — these are just a few of the youthful delights relived through these endearing snow babies. Bundled up for snuggly warmth, these chubby toddlers have charmed us with their antics since the early 1900's.*

Charts on page 92

HEARTFELT MESSAGES

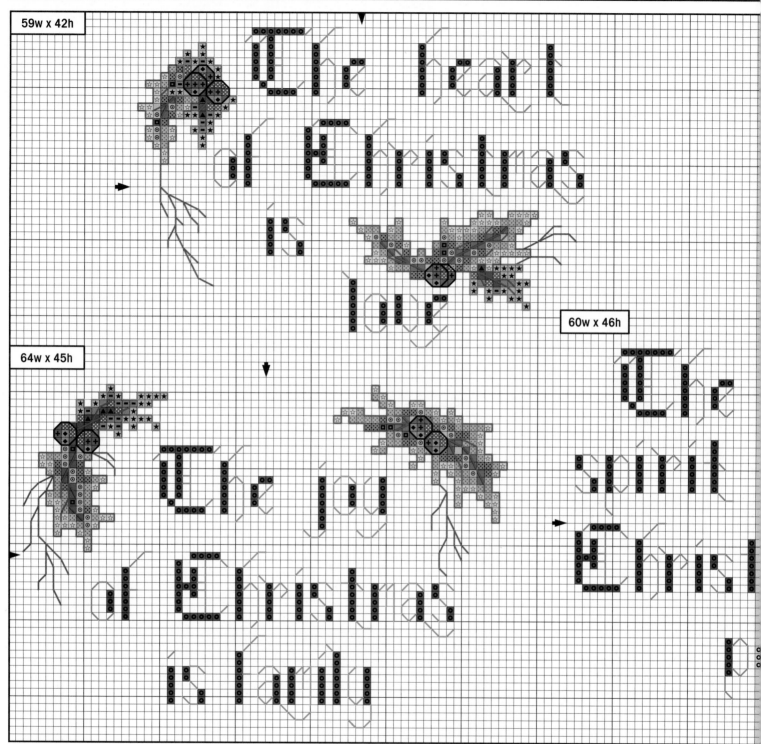

59w x 42h

64w x 45h

60w x 46h

Heartfelt Messages (shown on pages 6-7): Each design was stitched over 2 fabric threads on an 8" square of Cream Belfast Linen (32 ct). Two strands of floss were used for Cross Stitch and 1 strand for Backstitch.

For each ornament, you will need an 8" square of Cream Belfast Linen for backing, 10" x 5" piece of adhesive mounting board, tracing paper, pencil, 10" x 5" piece of batting, 2" x 18" bias fabric strip for cording, 18" length of ¼" dia. purchased cord, two 18" lengths of ¼"w ribbon for hanger, and clear-drying craft glue.

For pattern, fold tracing paper in half and place fold on dashed line of Heart Pattern, page 96; trace pattern onto tracing paper. Cut out pattern; unfold and press flat. Draw around pattern twice on mounting board and twice on batting; cut out. Remove paper from one piece of mounting board and press one batting piece onto mounting board. Repeat with remaining mounting board and batting.

Referring to photo, position pattern on wrong side of stitched piece; pin pattern in place. Cut stitched piece **1" larger** than pattern on all sides.

Cut backing fabric same size as stitched piece. Clip ½" into edge of stitched piece at ½" intervals. Center wrong side of stitched piece over batting on one mounting board piece; fold edges of stitched piece to back of mounting board and glue in place. For ornament back, repeat with backing fabric and remaining mounting board.

For cording, center cord on wrong side of bias strip; matching long edges, fold strip over cord. Use a zipper foot to baste along length of strip close to cord; trim seam allowance to ½". Beginning and ending at top center of stitched

50

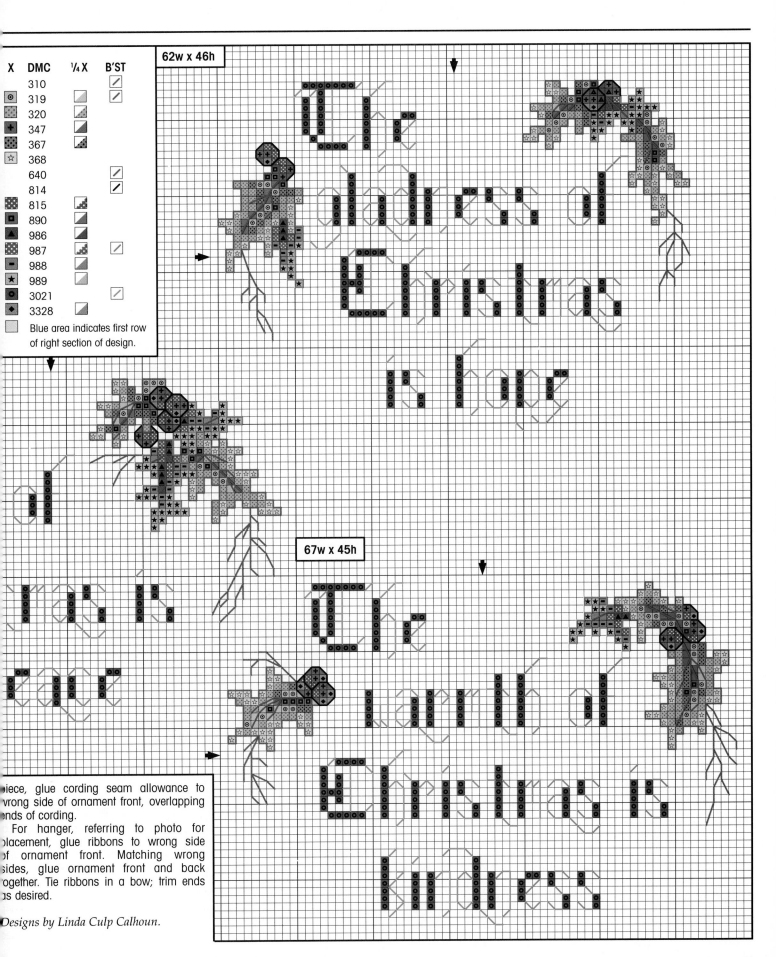

The chart legend:

X	DMC	1/4 X	B'ST
	310		/
⊙	319		/
	320		
+	347		
	367		
☆	368		
	640		/
	814		/
	815		
	890		
▲	986		
	987		/
-	988		
★	989		
⊙	3021		/
◆	3328		

Blue area indicates first row of right section of design.

62w x 46h

67w x 45h

piece, glue cording seam allowance to wrong side of ornament front, overlapping ends of cording.

For hanger, referring to photo for placement, glue ribbons to wrong side of ornament front. Matching wrong sides, glue ornament front and back together. Tie ribbons in a bow; trim ends as desired.

Designs by Linda Culp Calhoun.

heavenly host

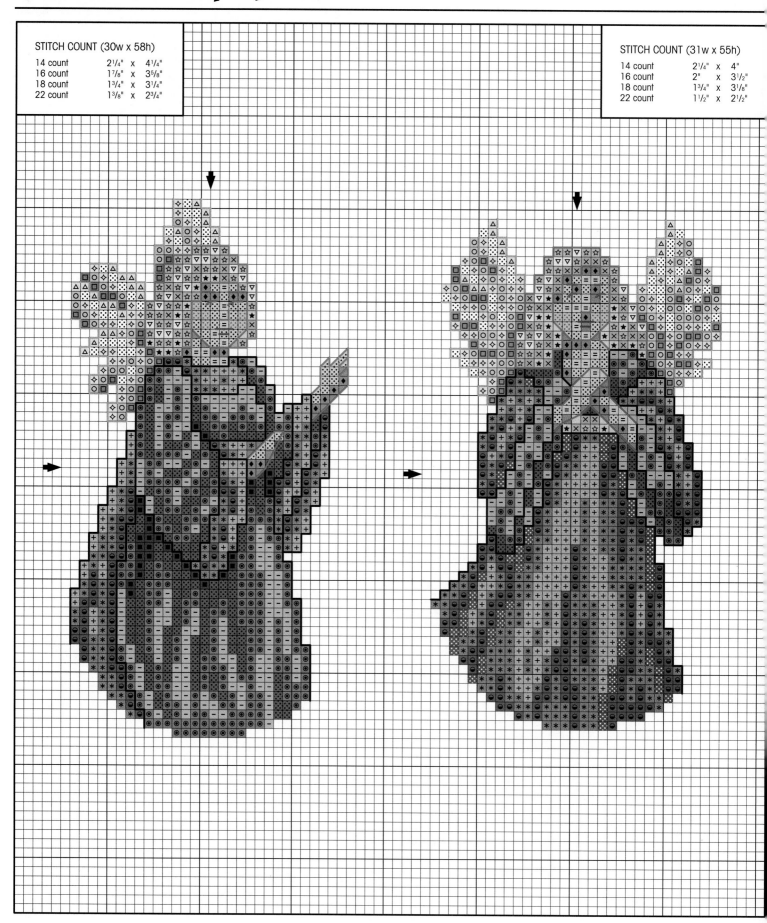

STITCH COUNT (30w x 58h)

14 count	2¼"	x	4¼"
16 count	1⅞"	x	3⅝"
18 count	1¾"	x	3¼"
22 count	1⅜"	x	2¾"

STITCH COUNT (31w x 55h)

14 count	2¼"	x	4"
16 count	2"	x	3½"
18 count	1¾"	x	3⅛"
22 count	1½"	x	2½"

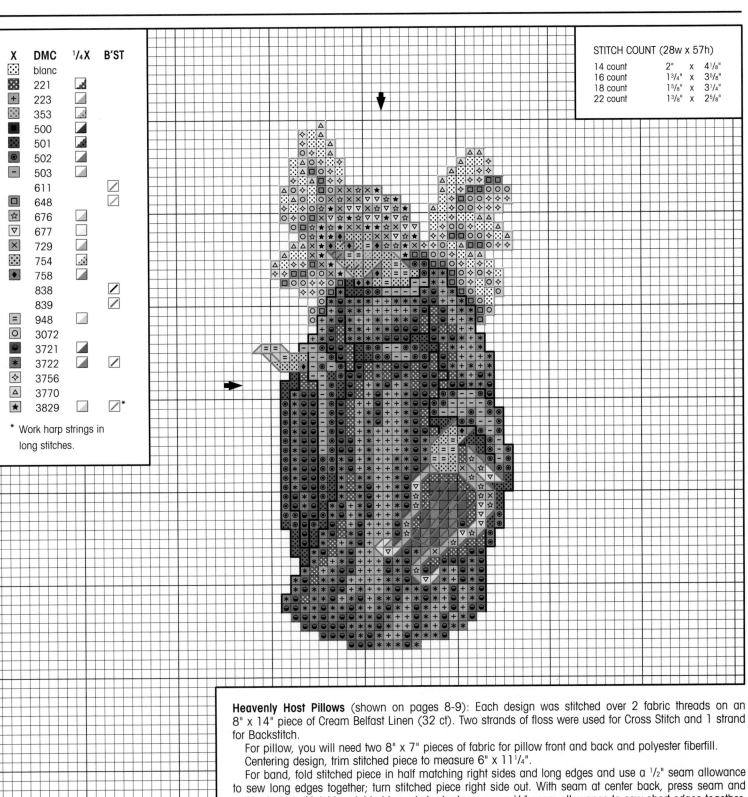

X	DMC	¼X	B'ST
▨	blanc		
▨	221	◩	
+	223	◩	
▨	353	◩	
■	500	◩	
▨	501	◩	
◉	502	◩	
-	503	◩	
	611		◪
▢	648		◪
☆	676	◩	
▽	677	◩	
✕	729	◩	
▨	754	◩	
◆	758	◩	
	838		◪
	839		◪
=	948	◩	
○	3072		
◨	3721	◩	
✳	3722	◩	◪
✧	3756	◩	
△	3770		
★	3829	◩	◪*

* Work harp strings in
long stitches.

STITCH COUNT (28w x 57h)

14 count	2"	x	4⅛"
16 count	1¾"	x	3⅝"
18 count	1⅝"	x	3¼"
22 count	1⅜"	x	2⅝"

Heavenly Host Pillows (shown on pages 8-9): Each design was stitched over 2 fabric threads on an 8" x 14" piece of Cream Belfast Linen (32 ct). Two strands of floss were used for Cross Stitch and 1 strand for Backstitch.

For pillow, you will need two 8" x 7" pieces of fabric for pillow front and back and polyester fiberfill. Centering design, trim stitched piece to measure 6" x 11¼".

For band, fold stitched piece in half matching right sides and long edges and use a ½" seam allowance to sew long edges together; turn stitched piece right side out. With seam at center back, press seam and stitched piece. Matching right side and short edges, use a ½" seam allowance to sew short edges together; press seam open and turn band right side out.

For pillow, match right sides and raw edges of pillow front and back. Leaving an opening for turning, use a ½" seam allowance to sew fabric pieces together; trim diagonally at corners. Turn pillow right side out, carefully pushing corners outward; stuff pillow lightly with polyester fiberfill and blind stitch opening closed.

Referring to photo, place band around pillow.

Needlework adaptations by Nancy Dockter.

the NIGHT BEFORE CHRISTMAS

Clock Face in Frame (shown on pages 11-13): The clock face design was stitched over 2 fabric threads on a 6" square of Cream Belfast Linen (32 ct). One strand of floss was used for Backstitch and French Knots. It was inserted in a purchased round gold frame (2½" dia. opening).

Referring to photo for placement, glue sprig of miniature holly, small wooden mouse, and red satin bow to frame.

The Night Before Christmas Pillows (shown on pages 11-13): Each design was stitched over 2 fabric threads on a 9" square of Light Mocha Belfast Linen (32 ct). Two strands of floss were used for Cross Stitch and 1 strand for Backstitch and French Knots.

To complete pillows, see **The Night Before Christmas Pillows**, page 57, for finishing instructions.

Designs by Holly DeFount of Kooler Design Studio.

63w x 49h

44w x 60h

42w x 64h

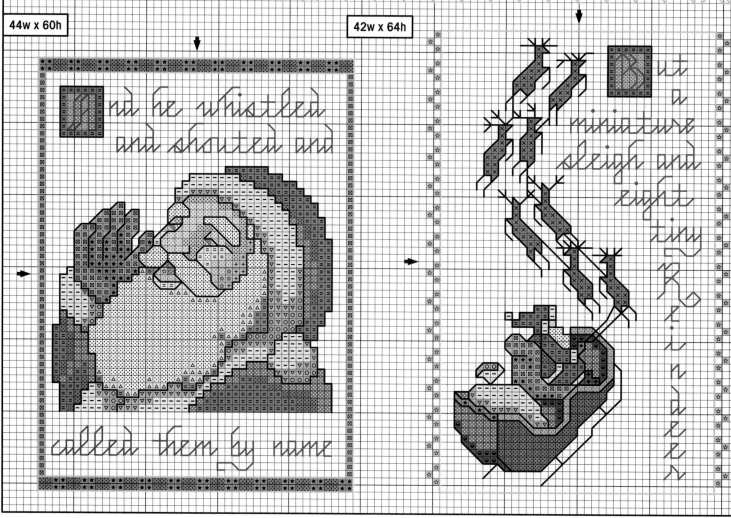

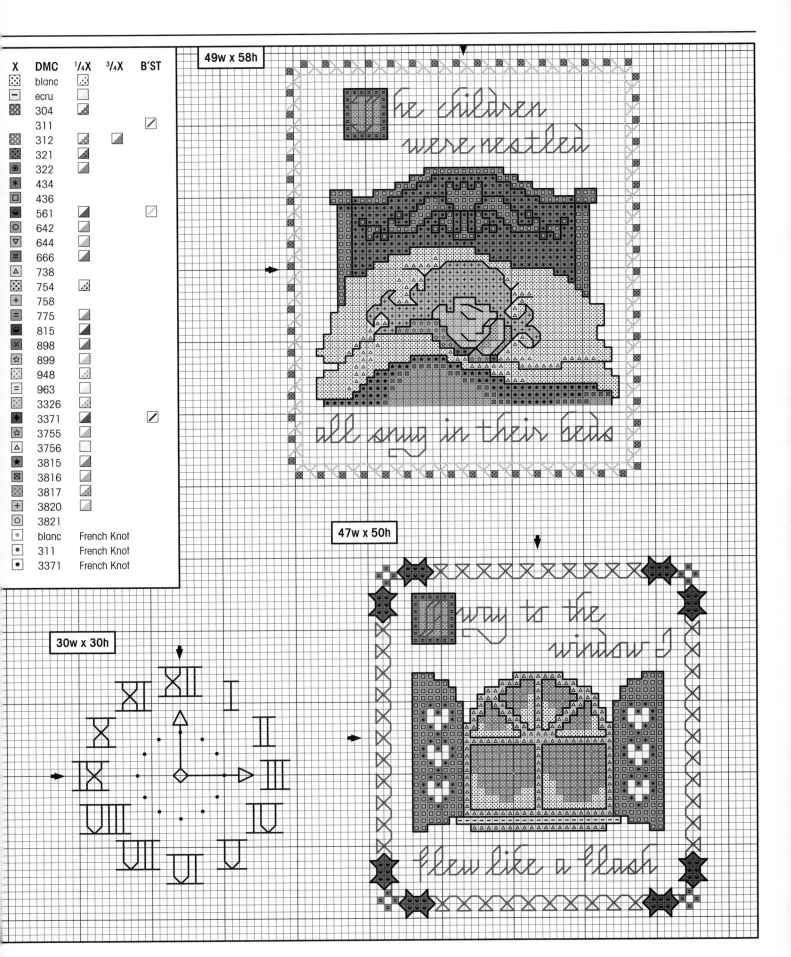

X	DMC	¼X	¾X	B'ST
⊡	blanc	⊡		
−	ecru	□		
▨	304	◪		
	311			◢
▨	312	◪	◩	
▨	321	◪		
◉	322	◩		
✳	434			
□	436			
◼	561	◩		◢
○	642	◩		
▽	644	◩		
=	666	◩		
△	738			
▨	754	◪		
✛	758			
=	775	◩		
◼	815	◩		
✕	898	◩		
☆	899	◩		
▨	948	◪		
=	963	◪		
▨	3326	◪		
✦	3371	◩		◢
☆	3755	◩		
△	3756	□		
★	3815	◩		
⊠	3816	◩		
▨	3817	◪		
✛	3820	◩		
⬠	3821			
◦	blanc	French Knot		
●	311	French Knot		
●	3371	French Knot		

49w x 58h

47w x 50h

30w x 30h

54w x 54h

With the sleigh full of toys and St. Nicholas, too.

56w x 36h

wink of his eye and a twist of his head

Designs by Holly DeFount of Kooler Design Studio.

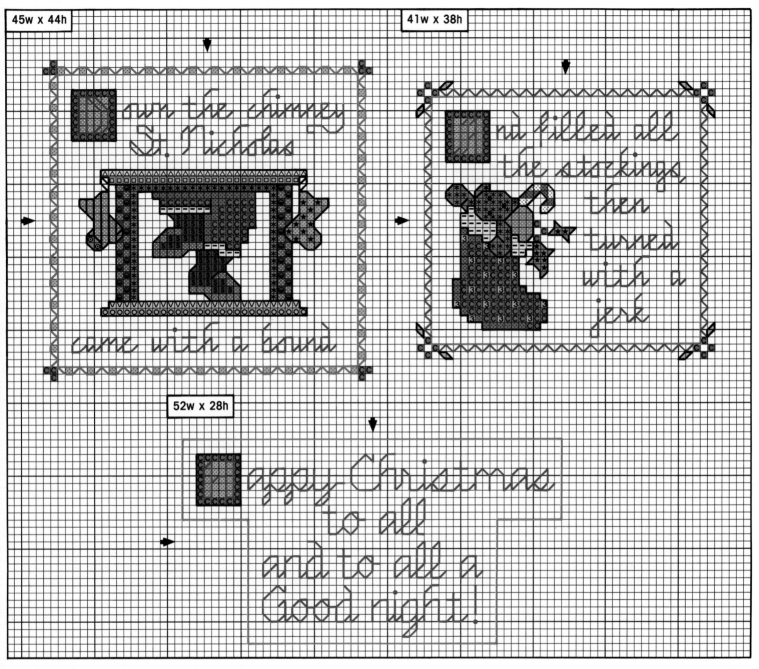

The Night Before Christmas Pillows (shown on pages 11-13): Each design was stitched over 2 fabric threads on a 9" square of Light Mocha Belfast Linen (32 ct). Two strands of floss were used for Cross Stitch and 1 strand for Backstitch and French Knots.

For each pillow, you will need a 9" square of Light Mocha Linen for backing, polyester fiberfill, and five 4 yd lengths of DMC 321 floss for twisted cord.

Matching right sides and raw edges, pin stitched piece and backing fabric together. Referring to photo, trim backing fabric and stitched piece 1" larger than design on all sides. Leaving an opening for turning, use a ½" seam allowance to sew pieces together; trim seam allowance diagonally at corners. Turn pillow right side out, carefully pushing corners outward. Stuff pillow with polyester fiberfill and blind stitch opening closed.

For twisted cord, place lengths of floss together and fold in half; tie a knot 2" from each end. Place the loop over a stationary object; pulling floss until taut, twist floss in a clockwise motion until tight. Holding floss at center to keep taut, fold floss in half matching knotted ends (Fig. 1). Release floss at fold; floss will twist together. Secure knotted ends by

tying an overhand knot. Pull cord through fingers to evenly distribute twists. Beginning and ending at bottom center of pillow, blind stitch twisted cord around edges of pillow.

Fig. 1

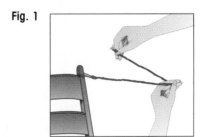

57

christmas perennials

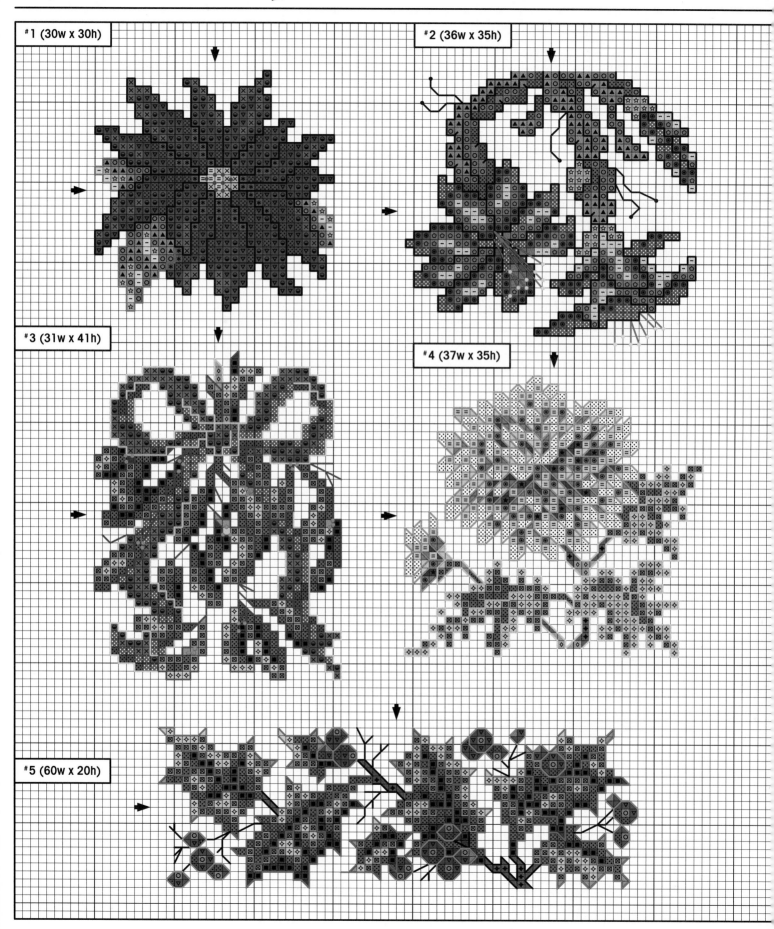

#1 (30w x 30h)

#2 (36w x 35h)

#3 (31w x 41h)

#4 (37w x 35h)

#5 (60w x 20h)

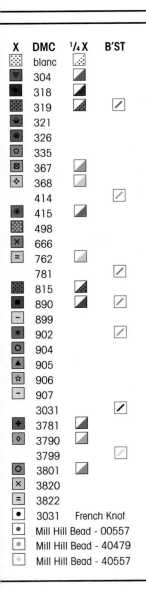

X	DMC	1/4 X	B'ST
	blanc		
	304		
	318		
	319		
	321		
	326		
	335		
	367		
	368		
	414		
	415		
	498		
	666		
	762		
	781		
	815		
	890		
	899		
	902		
	904		
	905		
	906		
	907		
	3031		
	3781		
	3790		
	3799		
	3801		
	3820		
	3822		
	3031	French Knot	
	Mill Hill Bead - 00557		
	Mill Hill Bead - 40479		
	Mill Hill Bead - 40557		

Poinsettia in Frame (shown on page 14): Design #1 was stitched over 2 fabric threads on an 8" square of Antique White Belfast Linen (32 ct). Two strands of floss were used for Cross Stitch and 1 strand for Backstitch. To attach beads, use 1 strand of DMC 676 floss; see Attaching Beads, page 94. It was inserted in a round gold frame (3 1/2" dia. opening).

White Mum Pillow (shown on page 14): Design #4 was stitched over 2 fabric threads on an 8" square of Antique White Belfast Linen (32 ct). Two strands of floss were used for Cross Stitch and 1 strand for Backstitch.

For pillow, you will need a 4 1/4" x 4" piece of Antique White Belfast Linen for backing, 2" x 16 1/2" bias fabric strip for cording, 16 1/2" length of 1/4" dia. purchased cord, and polyester fiberfill.

Centering design, trim stitched piece to measure 4 1/4" x 4".

Center cord on wrong side of bias strip; matching long edges, fold strip over cord. Use a zipper foot to baste along length of strip close to cord; trim seam allowance to 1/2". Matching raw edges, pin cording to right side of stitched piece and make a 3/8" clip in seam allowance of cording at corners. Ends of cording should overlap approximately 2"; pin overlapping end out of way. Starting 1" from beginning end of cording and ending 2 1/2" from overlapping end, baste cording to stitched piece. On overlapping end of cording, remove 2" of basting; fold end of fabric back and trim cord so that it meets beginning end of cord. Fold end of fabric 1/2" to wrong side; wrap fabric over beginning end of cording. Finish basting cording to stitched piece.

Matching right sides and leaving an opening for turning, use a 1/2" seam allowance to sew stitched piece and backing fabric together. Trim seam allowances to 1/4" and trim diagonally at corners; turn pillow right side out, carefully pushing corners outward. Stuff pillow with polyester fiberfill and blind stitch opening closed.

Christmas Cactus Shaker Box (shown on page 15): Design #2 was stitched over 2 fabric threads on an 8" square of Antique White Belfast Linen (32 ct). Two strands of floss were used for Cross Stitch and 1 strand for Backstitch and French Knots. To attach beads, use 1 strand of DMC blanc floss; see Attaching Petite Beads, page 73.

For Shaker box, you will need a 3" dia. round Shaker box, 3" dia. circle of batting for lid, 10" length of 5/8"w ribbon, 10" length of 1/2"w gold braid, fabric marking pencil, and clear-drying craft glue.

Centering design, trim stitched piece to a 4 1/2" dia. circle. Clip 1/4" into edge of stitched piece at 1" intervals. Glue batting on top of lid and place wrong side of stitched piece on batting; fold edge of stitched piece down and glue to side of lid. Referring to photo, glue ribbon and braid to side of lid.

Mistletoe Sachet (shown on page 15): Design #3 was stitched over 2 fabric threads on a 9" x 11" piece of Antique White Belfast Linen (32 ct). Two strands of floss were used for Cross Stitch and 1 strand for Backstitch. To attach beads, use 1 strand of DMC 895 floss; see Attaching Petite Beads, page 73.

For sachet, you will need a 4 1/4" x 6 3/4" piece of Antique White Belfast Linen for backing, 16" length of 1/16"w ribbon, 16" length of 1/16" dia. gold cord, polyester fiberfill, and scented oil.

Trim stitched piece to measure 4 1/4" x 6 3/4", allowing a 3" margin at top of design and 1 1/8" margins at sides and bottom of design.

Matching right sides and raw edges, use a 1/2" seam allowance to sew stitched piece and backing fabric together (backstitch at beginning and end of seam). Trim seam allowances diagonally at corners. Fringe top edge of sachet 1/2". Turn sachet right side out and stuff sachet with polyester fiberfill. Place a few drops of scented oil on a small amount of fiberfill and insert in middle of sachet. Tie ribbon and cord in a bow around sachet; tie overhand knots 1/2" from each end of cord and trim ribbon ends as desired.

Holly Cracker (shown on page 15): Design #5 was stitched over 2 fabric threads on 14" x 11" piece of Antique White Belfast Linen (32 ct). Two strands of floss were used for Cross Stitch and 1 strand for Backstitch.

For cracker, you will need a 15" x 6 1/2" piece of plaid fabric, 5" length of 1 1/2" dia. cardboard tube, two 9" lengths of 1/16"w ribbon, two 9" lengths of 1/8"w ribbon, two 9" lengths of 1/16" dia. gold cord, and fabric glue.

Centering design, trim stitched piece to measure 10" x 6 1/2". Fringe each short edge of stitched piece 1/2".

Press each short edge of fabric 2" to wrong side; glue in place. With stitched piece centered, place wrong side of stitched piece on right side of fabric. Glue one long edge of stitched piece to one long edge of fabric; repeat with remaining long edges; allow glue to dry. Press one long edge of stitched piece and fabric 1/2" to wrong side; glue in place. Insert candy or small gift into tube and center tube lengthwise on wrong side of fabric and stitched piece. Glue unpressed edge of fabric and stitched piece to tube. Wrap fabric and stitched piece smoothly around tube; glue pressed edge in place. Referring to photo, tie a bow at each end of stitched piece with one length of each ribbon and one length of gold cord; tie overhand knots 1/2" from each end of cord and trim ribbon ends as desired.

Designs and needlework adaptation by Nancy Dockter.

quilts of the bible

Quilts of the Bible (shown on pages 16-17): Each design was stitched on a 7" square of Dirty Aida (16 ct). Two strands of floss were used for Cross Stitch and 1 strand for Backstitch.

For each ornament, you will need two 5" squares of wool fabric, two 5" squares of fusible web, and a 5" length of ⅛"w ribbon, for hanger.

Center one square of fusible web on wrong side of one square of wool fabric; center wrong side of remaining square of wool fabric on fusible web. Following manufacturer's directions, fuse wool squares together. Trim stitched piece five squares larger than design on all sides; fringe to within one square of design. Trim remaining square of fusible web slightly smaller than cross-stitched design area; center fusible web on wool fabric and center wrong side of stitched piece on fusible web. Fuse stitched piece to wool fabric. Trim edges of wool fabric with pinking shears ⅜" from edge of fringe.

For hanger, fold ribbon in half; referring to photo, tack ends to back of ornament.

Designs by Kathy Elrod.

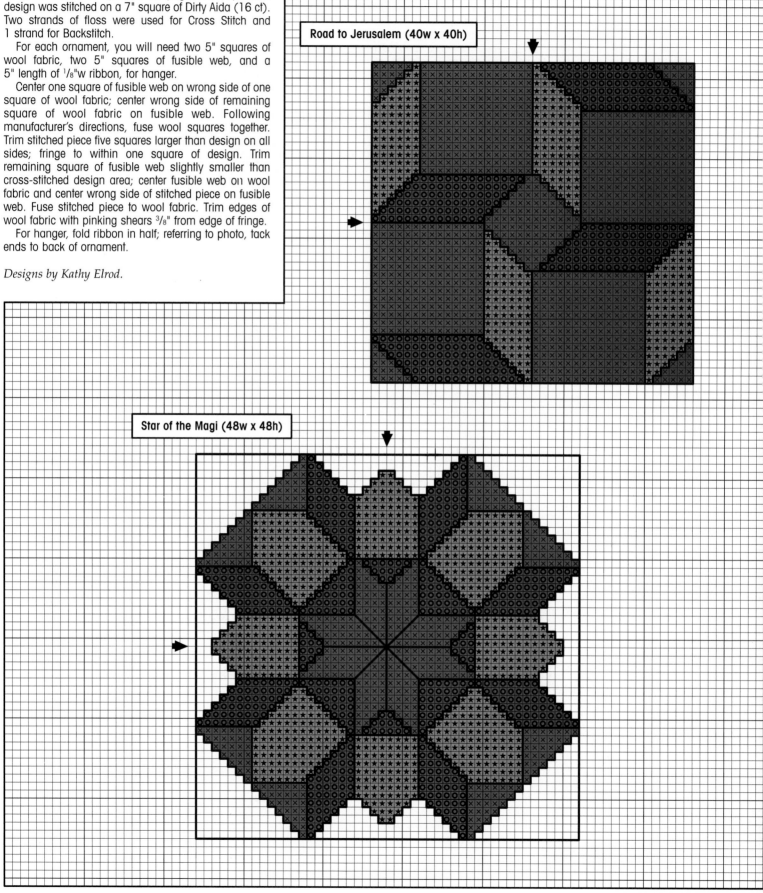

Road to Jerusalem (40w x 40h)

Star of the Magi (48w x 48h)

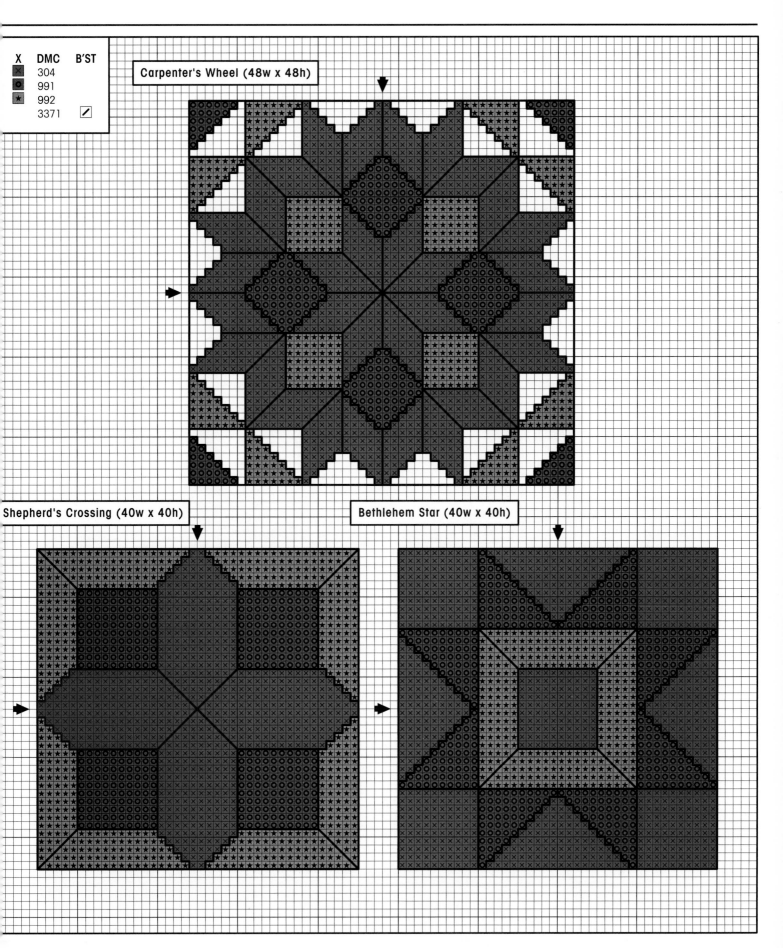

X	DMC	B'ST
▨	304	
◉	991	
★	992	
	3371	◪

Carpenter's Wheel (48w x 48h)

Shepherd's Crossing (40w x 40h)

Bethlehem Star (40w x 40h)

good cheer elves

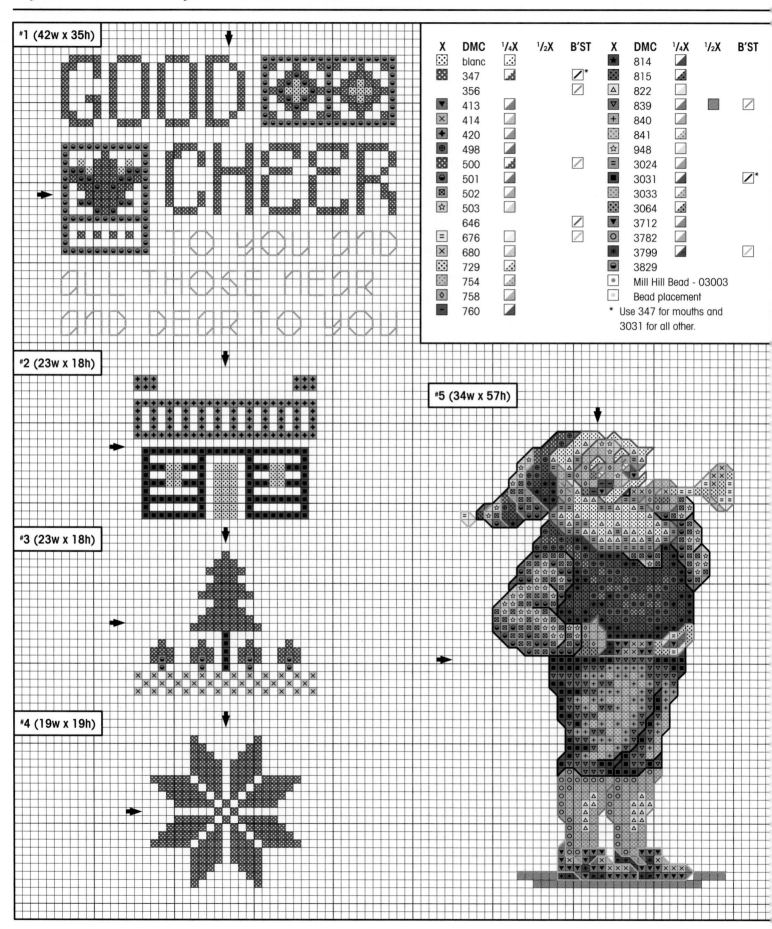

#1 (42w x 35h)

GOOD CHEER

TO YOU AND ALL THOSE NEAR AND DEAR TO YOU

#2 (23w x 18h)

#3 (23w x 18h)

#4 (19w x 19h)

#5 (34w x 57h)

X	DMC	¼X	½X	B'ST	X	DMC	¼X	½X	B'ST
	blanc				★	814			
	347			*		815			
	356					822			
▼	413				▽	839			
✕	414				+	840			
✦	420					841			
⊕	498				☆	948			
	500				=	3024			
◉	501				■	3031			*
✕	502					3033			
☆	503					3064			
	646				▼	3712			
=	676				○	3782			
✕	680				✱	3799			
	729				◉	3829			
	754				•	Mill Hill Bead - 03003			
◇	758					Bead placement			
	760								

* Use 347 for mouths and 3031 for all other.

#6 (26w x 43h)

"Good Cheer" Pillow (shown on page 18): Design #1 was stitched on a 10" x 9" piece of Fiddler's Lite (14 ct). Three strands of floss were used for Cross Stitch and 1 strand for Backstitch.

Centering design, trim stitched piece to measure 5¹/₂" x 5". To complete pillow, see "Good Cheer" Pillow Finishing, page 87.

Mini Log Carriers (shown on pages 19-21): Designs #2, #3, and #4 were each stitched on a 7" x 11" piece of Fiddler's Lite (14 ct) with top of design 3¹/₂" from one short edge. Three strands of floss were used for Cross Stitch.

Centering design horizontally and leaving a 1¹/₂" margin at top of design, trim stitched piece to measure 3¹/₄" x 7¹/₄". To complete log carrier, see Mini Log Carrier Finishing, page 87.

Twig-Framed Elves (shown on pages 19-21): Designs #5, #7, and #8 were each stitched on a 7" x 9" piece of Fiddler's Lite (14 ct). Three strands of floss were used for Cross Stitch and 1 strand for Half Cross Stitch and Backstitch. To attach beads, use 1 strand of DMC 498 floss; see Attaching Beads, page 94. To complete ornament, see Twig-Framed Elf Finishing, page 87.

Stiffened Mushrooms (shown on pages 19-21): Design #6 was stitched on a 6" x 7" piece of Fiddler's Lite (14 ct). Three strands of floss were used for Cross Stitch and 1 strand for Backstitch.

For each mushroom, you will need a 6" x 7" piece of lightweight cream fabric for backing, fabric stiffener, small foam brush, eight 4mm ivory beads, and clear-drying craft glue.

Apply a heavy coat of fabric stiffener to back of stitched piece using small foam brush. Matching wrong sides, place stitched piece on backing fabric, smoothing stitched piece while pressing fabric pieces together; allow to dry. Apply fabric stiffener to backing fabric; allow to dry. Cut out close to edges of stitched design. Referring to chart for placement, glue beads to mushroom.

Designs by Nancy Dockter.

#7 (31w x 56h)   **#8 (28w x 57h)**

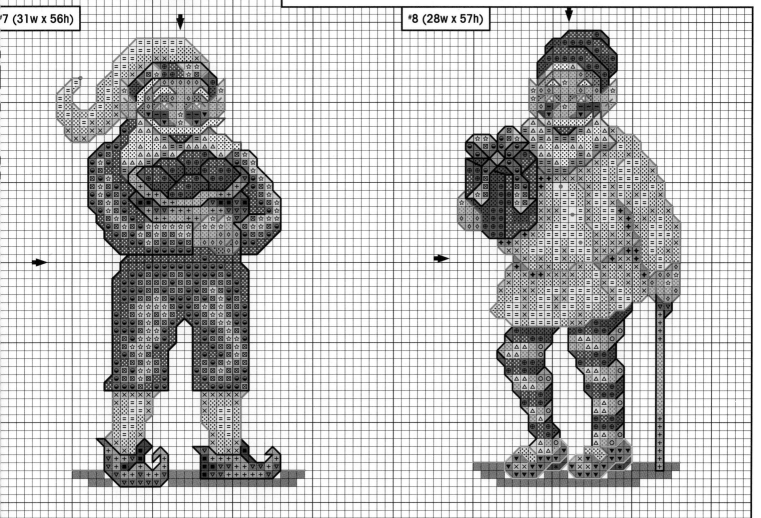

YOUNG AT HEART

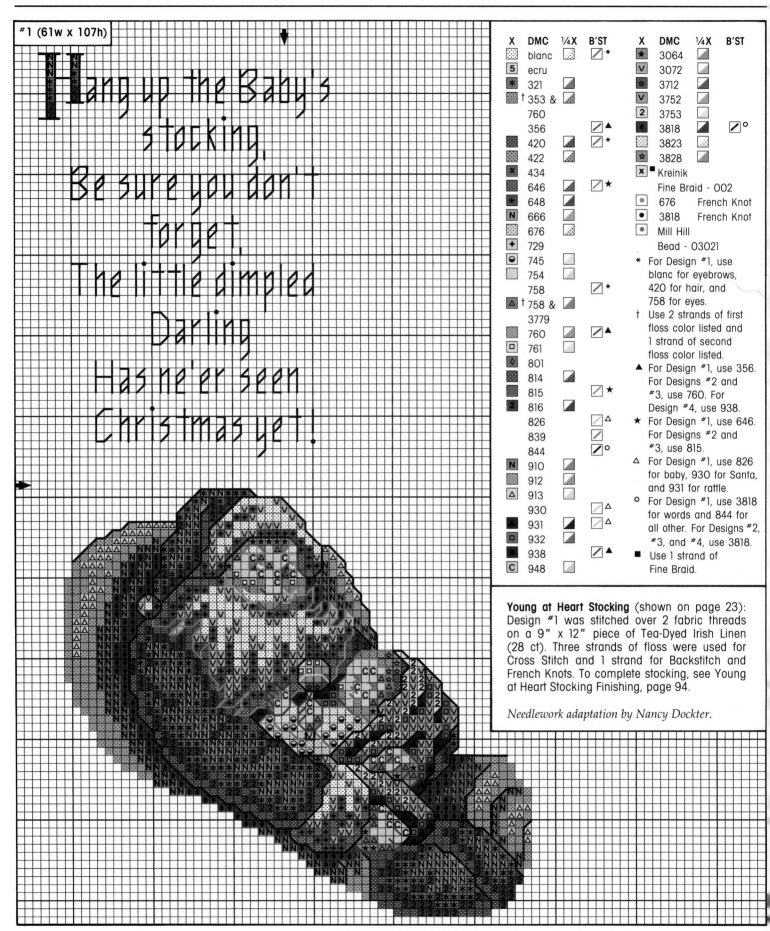

#1 (61w x 107h)

Hang up the Baby's stocking,
Be sure you don't forget,
The little dimpled Darling
Has ne'er seen Christmas yet!

X	DMC	¼X	B'ST		X	DMC	¼X	B'ST
	blanc		∕ *		★	3064	∕	
5	ecru				V	3072	∕	
*	321				☆	3712	∕	
†	353 &	∕			V	3752	∕	
	760				2	3753	∕	
	356		∕ ▲		◆	3818	∕	∕ °
	420	∕	∕ *			3823		∕
	422	∕			☆	3828	∕	
X	434		∕		x ■	Kreinik		
	646	∕	∕ ★			Fine Braid - 002		
◆	648	∕			●	676	French Knot	
N	666	∕			●	3818	French Knot	
	676	∕			●	Mill Hill		
◆	729					Bead - 03021		
⊙	745	∕						
	754	∕						
	758		∕ *					
▲ †	758 &	∕						
	3779							
	760	∕	∕ ▲					
▢	761	∕						
◇	801	∕						
	814	∕						
	815	∕	∕ ★					
2	816	∕						
	826	∕	∕ △					
	839	∕						
	844		∕ °					
N	910	∕						
	912	∕						
△	913	∕						
	930		∕ △					
■	931	∕	∕ △					
▢	932	∕						
■	938	∕	∕ ▲					
C	948	∕						

* For Design #1, use blanc for eyebrows, 420 for hair, and 758 for eyes.

† Use 2 strands of first floss color listed and 1 strand of second floss color listed.

▲ For Design #1, use 356. For Designs #2 and #3, use 760. For Design #4, use 938.

★ For Design #1, use 646. For Designs #2 and #3, use 815.

△ For Design #1, use 826 for baby, 930 for Santa, and 931 for rattle.

° For Design #1, use 3818 for words and 844 for all other. For Designs #2, #3, and #4, use 3818.

■ Use 1 strand of Fine Braid.

Young at Heart Stocking (shown on page 23): Design #1 was stitched over 2 fabric threads on a 9" x 12" piece of Tea-Dyed Irish Linen (28 ct). Three strands of floss were used for Cross Stitch and 1 strand for Backstitch and French Knots. To complete stocking, see Young at Heart Stocking Finishing, page 94.

Needlework adaptation by Nancy Dockter.

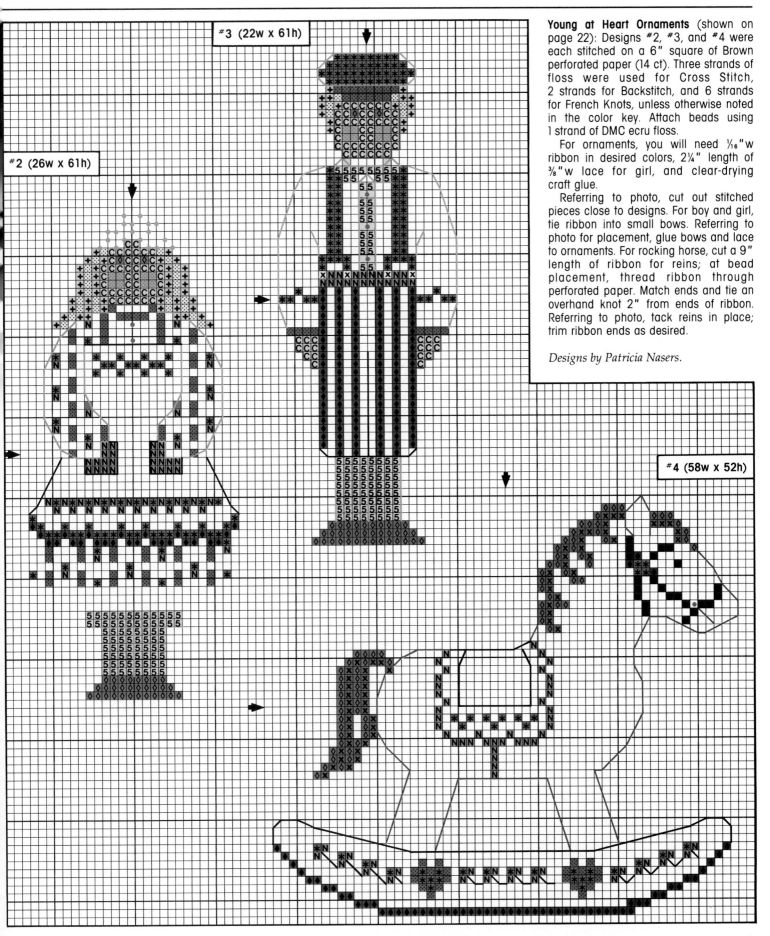

#3 (22w x 61h)

#2 (26w x 61h)

Young at Heart Ornaments (shown on page 22): Designs #2, #3, and #4 were each stitched on a 6" square of Brown perforated paper (14 ct). Three strands of floss were used for Cross Stitch, 2 strands for Backstitch, and 6 strands for French Knots, unless otherwise noted in the color key. Attach beads using 1 strand of DMC ecru floss.

For ornaments, you will need 1/16"w ribbon in desired colors, 2¼" length of 3/8"w lace for girl, and clear-drying craft glue.

Referring to photo, cut out stitched pieces close to designs. For boy and girl, tie ribbon into small bows. Referring to photo for placement, glue bows and lace to ornaments. For rocking horse, cut a 9" length of ribbon for reins; at bead placement, thread ribbon through perforated paper. Match ends and tie an overhand knot 2" from ends of ribbon. Referring to photo, tack reins in place; trim ribbon ends as desired.

Designs by Patricia Nasers.

#4 (58w x 52h)

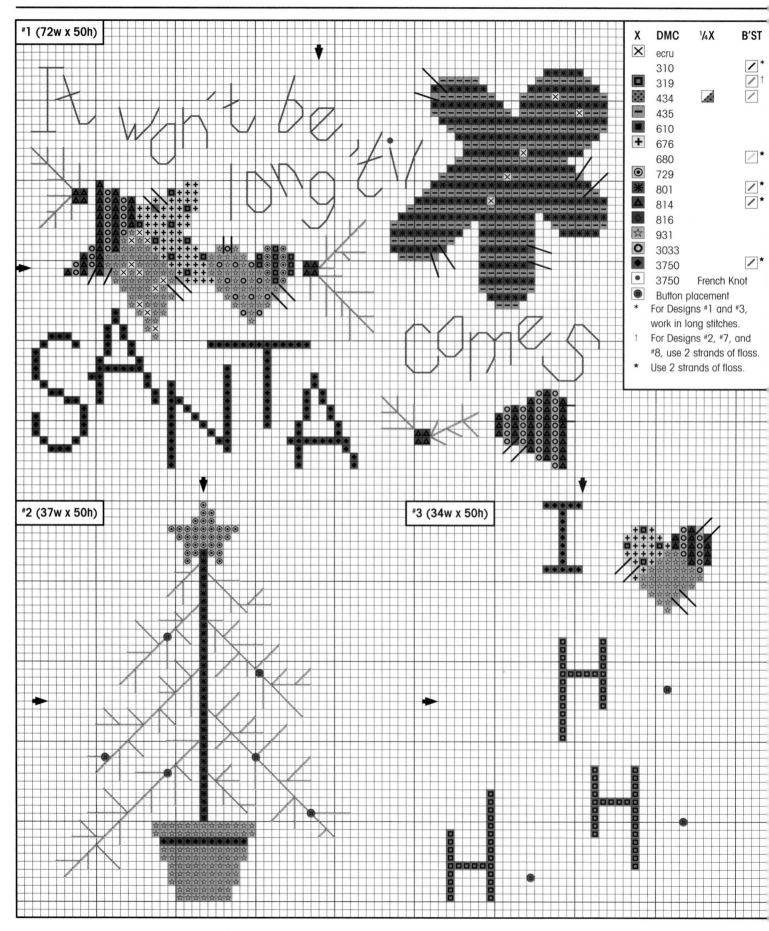

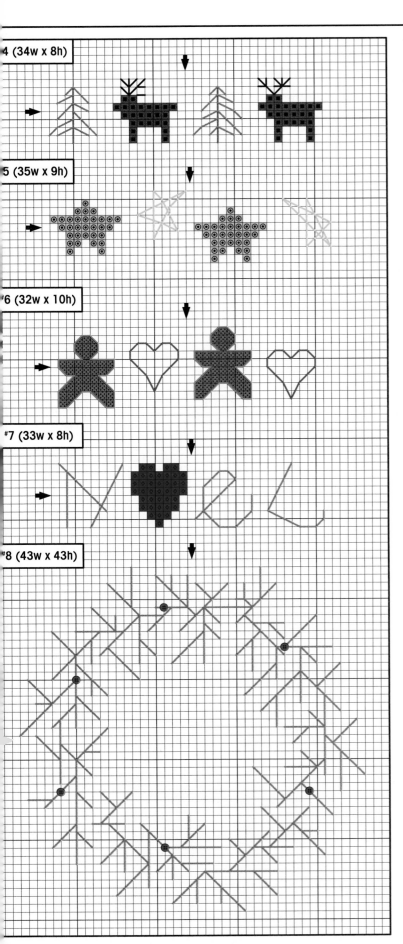

"It Won't Be Long" Ornament (shown on page 24): Design #1 was stitched over 2 fabric threads on a 9" x 8" piece of Light Mocha Cashel Linen (28 ct). Three strands of floss were used for Cross Stitch, 1 strand for Backstitch, 2 strands for French Knot, and 4 strands for Blanket Stitch, unless otherwise noted in the color key.

For ornament, you will need a 6" x 4½" piece of lightweight cream fabric for backing, 6¼" x 4¾" piece of natural batting, DMC 642 floss for Blanket Stitch, two 6" lengths of #20 jute twine, and 8" stick for hanger.

Centering design, trim stitched piece to measure 6" x 4½". To complete ornament, see Blanket-Stitched Ornament Finishing, page 94.

Tree Ornament (shown on page 25): Design #2 was stitched over 2 fabric threads on a 7" x 8" piece of Light Mocha Cashel Linen (28 ct). Three strands of floss were used for Cross Stitch, 2 strands for Backstitch, and 4 strands for Blanket Stitch.

For ornament, you will need a 3½" x 4½" piece of lightweight cream fabric for backing, 3¾" x 4¾" piece of natural batting, DMC 642 floss for Blanket Stitch, two 6" lengths of #20 jute twine, 5½" stick for hanger, and 6 assorted buttons.

Centering design, trim stitched piece to measure 3½" x 4½". To complete ornament, see Blanket-Stitched Ornament Finishing, page 94.

Stocking Ornament (shown on page 25): Design #3 was stitched over 2 fabric threads on a 7" x 8" piece of Light Mocha Cashel Linen (28 ct). Three strands of floss were used for Cross Stitch, 1 strand for Backstitch, and 4 strands for Blanket Stitch.

For ornament, you will need a 7" x 8" piece of lightweight cream fabric for backing, 7" x 8" piece of natural batting, tracing paper, pencil, DMC 642 floss for Blanket Stitch, 5" length of #20 jute twine, fabric marking pencil, and 3 assorted buttons.

Trace Schoolgirl Stocking Pattern, page 96, onto tracing paper; cut out pattern. Referring to photo, position pattern on wrong side of stitched piece; pin pattern in place. Use fabric marking pencil to draw around pattern; remove pattern and cut out on drawn line. Use pattern and cut one from backing fabric. Adding ⅛" to all sides, use pattern and cut one from batting. To complete ornament, see Blanket-Stitched Ornament Finishing, page 94.

Wreath Ornament (shown on page 25): Design #8 was stitched over 2 fabric threads on an 8" square of Light Mocha Cashel Linen (28 ct). Two strands of floss were used for Backstitch and 4 strands for Blanket Stitch.

For ornament, you will need a 4" dia. circle of lightweight cream fabric for backing, 4¼" dia. circle of natural batting, DMC 642 floss for Blanket Stitch, 5" length of #20 jute twine, and 6 assorted buttons.

Centering design, trim stitched piece to a 4" dia. circle. To complete ornament, see Blanket-Stitched Ornament Finishing, page 94.

Spool Ornaments (shown on page 25): Designs #4, #5, #6, and #7 were each stitched over 2 fabric threads on a 6" x 4" piece of Light Mocha Cashel Linen (28 ct). Three strands of floss were used for Cross Stitch, 1 strand for Backstitch, and 4 strands for Blanket Stitch, unless otherwise noted in the color key.

For each ornament, you will need a 1⅞" wooden waisted spool, wood stain, DMC 642 floss for Blanket Stitch, ⅜" dia. bead, and 22" length of #20 jute twine.

Centering design, trim stitched piece to measure 3¾" x 2".

Apply wood stain to spool; allow to dry. Press long edges of stitched piece ½" to wrong side. Starting ½" from one short edge, Blanket Stitch pressed edge to within ½" of opposite end; see Blanket Stitch Instructions, page 93. Repeat for remaining long edge. Press one short edge ½" to wrong side. Wrap stitched piece around spool and whipstitch in place.

For hanger, thread jute through spool, bead, and then back through spool. Referring to photo, tie ends of jute in bow; trim ends as desired.

Designs by Jane Chandler.

67

paper doll teddy

48w x 74h

31w x 34h

50w x 60h

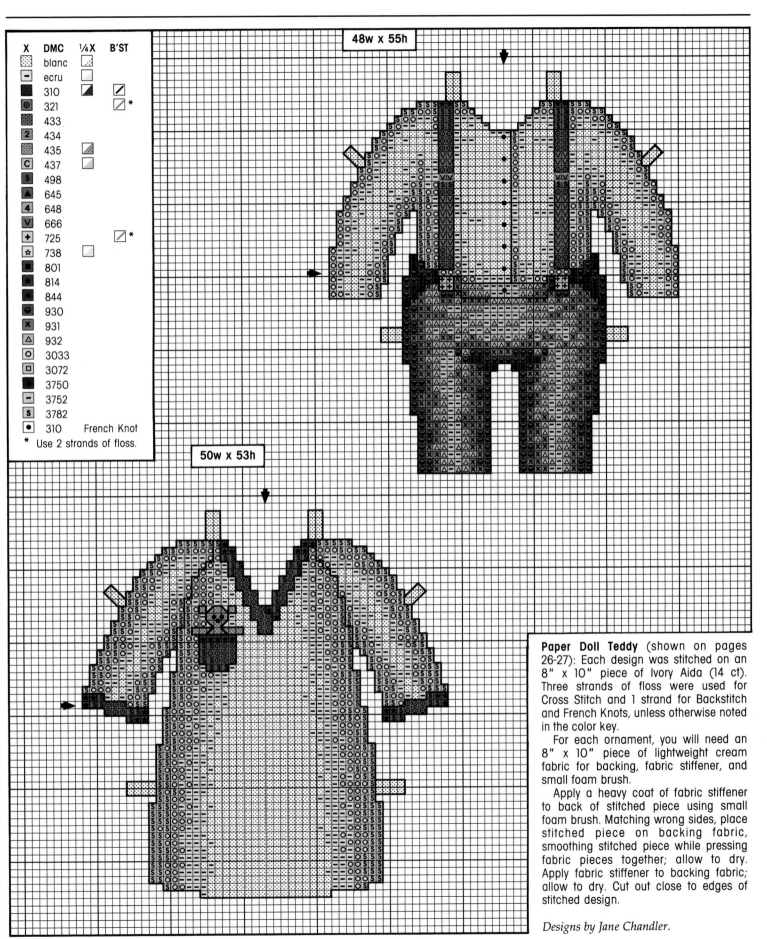

X	DMC	¼X	B'ST
	blanc		
-	ecru		
	310		/ *
⊙	321		
	433		
2	434		
	435		
C	437		
S	498		
▲	645		
4	648		
V	666		
+	725		/ *
☆	738		
	801		
★	814		
	844		
⊙	930		
X	931		
△	932		
○	3033		
□	3072		
	3750		
-	3752		
S	3782		
●	310	French Knot	

* Use 2 strands of floss.

48w x 55h

50w x 53h

Paper Doll Teddy (shown on pages 26-27): Each design was stitched on an 8" x 10" piece of Ivory Aida (14 ct). Three strands of floss were used for Cross Stitch and 1 strand for Backstitch and French Knots, unless otherwise noted in the color key.

For each ornament, you will need an 8" x 10" piece of lightweight cream fabric for backing, fabric stiffener, and small foam brush.

Apply a heavy coat of fabric stiffener to back of stitched piece using small foam brush. Matching wrong sides, place stitched piece on backing fabric, smoothing stitched piece while pressing fabric pieces together; allow to dry. Apply fabric stiffener to backing fabric; allow to dry. Cut out close to edges of stitched design.

Designs by Jane Chandler.

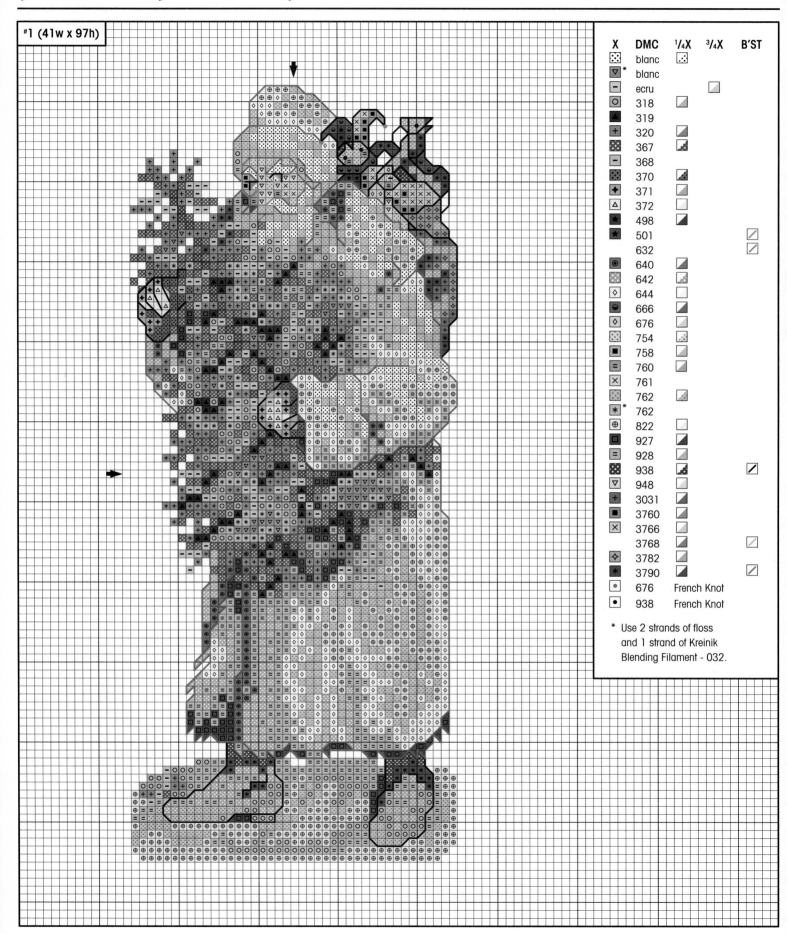

#1 (41w x 97h)

X	DMC	¼X	¾X	B'ST
⊠	blanc	⊠		
▽ *	blanc			
-	ecru		◢	
⊙	318	◢		
◼	319			
+	320	◢		
⊠	367	◢		
-	368			
⊠	370	◢		
◆	371	◢		
△	372	◻		
★	498	◢		
★	501			◿
	632			◿
◉	640	◢		
⊠	642	◢		
◇	644	◢		
◙	666	◢		
◇	676	◢		
⊠	754	◢		
◼	758	◢		
=	760	◢		
⊠	761			
⊠	762	◢		
✳ *	762			
⊕	822	◻		
◻	927	◢		
=	928	◢		
⊠	938	◢		◿
▽	948	◢		
+	3031	◢		
◼	3760	◢		
⊠	3766	◢		
	3768	◢		◿
◈	3782	◢		
✳	3790	◢		◿
•	676	French Knot		
●	938	French Knot		

* Use 2 strands of floss
and 1 strand of Kreinik
Blending Filament - 032.

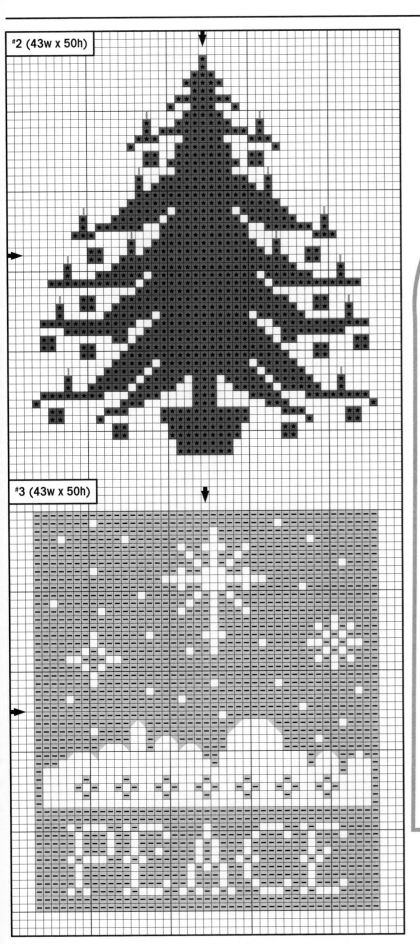

#2 (43w x 50h)

#3 (43w x 50h)

White Coat Santa (shown on page 30): Design #1 was stitched over 2 fabric threads on a 9" x 12" piece of Cream Irish Linen (32 ct). Two strands of floss were used for Cross Stitch and 1 strand for Backstitch and French Knots, unless otherwise noted in the color key.

For ornament, you will need a 9" x 12" piece of Cream Irish Linen for backing, 9" x 8" piece of adhesive mounting board, tracing paper, pencil, 9" x 8" piece of batting, 25" length of 3/8" dia. purchased cording with attached seam allowance, and clear-drying craft glue.

Trace pattern onto tracing paper; cut out pattern. Draw around pattern twice on mounting board and twice on batting; cut out. Remove paper from one piece of mounting board and press one batting piece onto mounting board. Repeat with remaining mounting board and batting.

Referring to photo, position pattern on wrong side of stitched piece; pin pattern in place. Cut stitched piece **1" larger** than pattern on all sides. Cut backing fabric same size as stitched piece. Clip 1/2" into curved edge of stitched piece at 1/2" intervals. Center wrong side of stitched piece over batting on one mounting board piece; fold edges of stitched piece to back of mounting board and glue in place. For ornament back, repeat with backing fabric and remaining mounting board.

Beginning and ending at bottom center of stitched piece, glue cording seam allowance to wrong side of ornament front, overlapping ends of cording. Matching wrong sides, glue ornament front and back together.

Needlework adaptation by Donna Vermillion Giampa.

Corded Tree Ornament (shown on page 28): Design #2 was stitched on a 9" x 10" piece of Ivory Aida (14 ct). Four strands of floss were used for Cross Stitch and 2 strands for Backstitch. To complete ornament, see Corded Ornament Finishing below.

Corded Peace Ornament (shown on page 28): Design #3 was stitched on a 9" x 10" piece of Teal Green Aida (14 ct). Four strands of floss were used for Cross Stitch. To complete ornament, see Corded Ornament Finishing below.

Designs by Linda Culp Calhoun.

CORDED ORNAMENT FINISHING

For each ornament, you will need a 5 1/8" x 5 5/8" piece of Aida for backing (same color as stitched piece), two 3 5/8" x 4 1/8" pieces of adhesive mounting board, two 3 5/8" x 4 1/8" pieces of batting, 19" length of 1/4" dia. purchased cording with attached seam allowance, and clear-drying craft glue.

Centering design, trim stitched piece to measure 5 1/8" x 5 5/8".

Remove paper from one piece of mounting board and press one batting piece onto mounting board. Repeat with remaining mounting board and batting.

Center wrong side of stitched piece over batting on one mounting board piece; fold edges of stitched piece to back of mounting board and glue in place. For ornament back, repeat with backing fabric and remaining mounting board.

Beginning and ending at bottom center of stitched piece, glue cording seam allowance to wrong side of ornament front, overlapping ends of cording. Matching wrong sides, glue ornament front and back together.

PRETTY SAMPLING

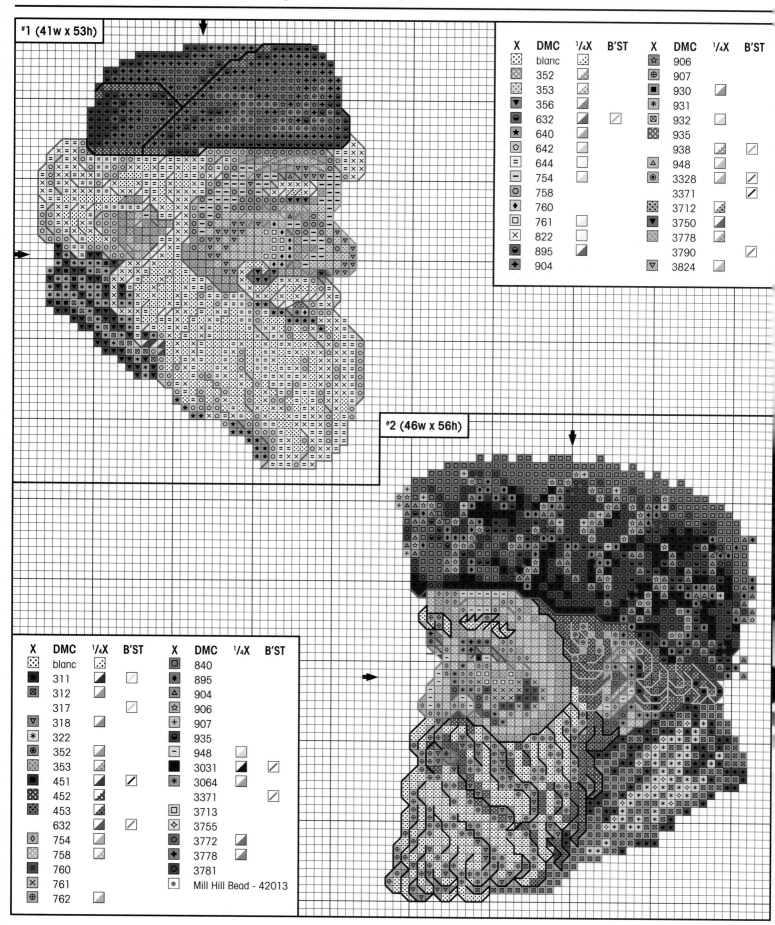

#1 (41w x 53h)

X	DMC	¼X	B'ST	X	DMC	¼X	B'ST
	blanc				906		
	352				907		
	353				930		
	356				931		
	632				932		
	640				935		
	642				938		
	644				948		
	754				3328		
	758				3371		
	760				3712		
	761				3750		
	822				3778		
	895				3790		
	904				3824		

#2 (46w x 56h)

X	DMC	¼X	B'ST	X	DMC	¼X	B'ST
	blanc				840		
	311				895		
	312				904		
	317				906		
	318				907		
	322				935		
	352				948		
	353				3031		
	451				3064		
	452				3371		
	453				3713		
	632				3755		
	754				3772		
	758				3778		
	760				3781		
	761				Mill Hill Bead - 42013		
	762						

X	DMC	¼X	B'ST
⊡	blanc	⊡	
★	319	◢	
✕	321	◢	
⊙	610	◢	
▦	611	◪	
	647		◹
⊡	648	◪	
☆ *	722 &		
	3340		
⊕	745		
=	746		
▲	816	◢	
▣	869	◢	
	934		◹
+	945		
▦	986	◪	
▼	987	◢	
◇	3023	◢	
	3031	◪	◹
▲	3032	◢	
■	3072	▢	
–	3347	◹	
✳	3781	◢	◹
◉	3801	◢	
⊡	3823	⊡	
○	3825	◢	
▽	3828	◹	

* Use 2 strands of first
  floss color listed and
  1 strand of second
  floss color listed.

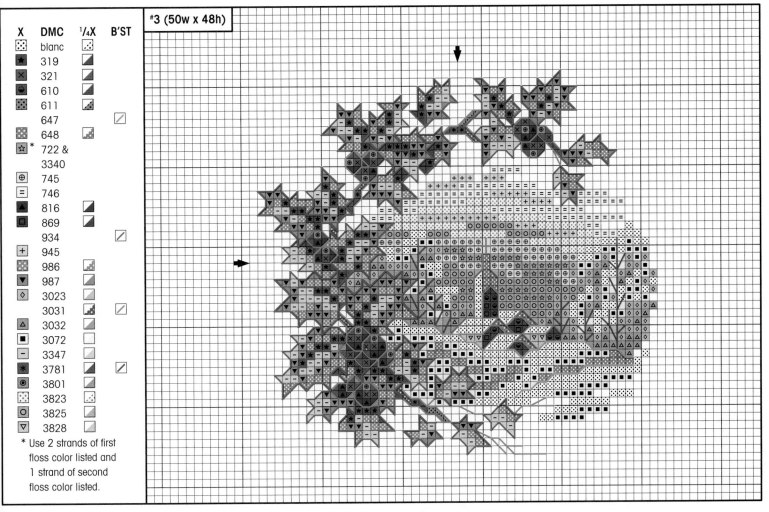

#3 (50w x 48h)

Santa Profiles (shown on page 31): Designs #1 and #2 were each stitched over 2 fabric threads on a 9" square of Tea-Dyed Irish Linen (28 ct). Three strands of floss were used for Cross Stitch and 1 strand for Backstitch. To attach beads, use 1 strand of DMC 3781 floss; see Attaching Petite Beads below.

For each ornament, you will need a 9" square of Tea-Dyed Irish Linen for backing and polyester fiberfill.

Matching right sides and raw edges, pin stitched piece and backing fabric together. Leaving an opening for turning and stuffing, sew backing fabric to stitched piece ¼" away from edge of design. Trim seam allowance to ¼" and clip curves; turn right side out. Stuff ornament lightly with polyester fiberfill and blind stitch opening closed.

Needlework adaptations by
Vicky D'Agostino, Victoria's Needle.

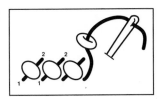

ATTACHING PETITE BEADS
Refer to chart for bead placement and sew bead in place using a fine needle that will pass through bead. Bring needle up at 1, run needle through bead then down at 2. Secure floss on back or move to next bead as shown in **Fig. 1**.

Christmas Village (shown on page 31): Design #3 was stitched over 2 fabric threads on an 8" square of Tea-Dyed Irish Linen (28 ct). Three strands of floss were used for Cross Stitch and 1 strand for Backstitch.

For ornament, you will need a 6¼" dia. circle of Tea-Dyed Irish Linen for backing, two 4¼" dia. circles of adhesive mounting board, two 4¼" dia. circles of batting, 17" length of ⅜" dia. purchased cording with attached seam allowance, and clear-drying craft glue.

Centering design, trim stitched piece to a 6¼" dia. circle.

Remove paper from one piece of mounting board and press one batting piece onto mounting board. Repeat with remaining mounting board and batting.

Clip ½" into edge of stitched piece at ½" intervals. Center wrong side of stitched piece over batting on one mounting board piece; fold edges of stitched piece to back of mounting board and glue in place. For ornament back, repeat with backing fabric and remaining mounting board.

Beginning and ending at bottom center of stitched piece, glue cording seam allowance to wrong side of ornament front, overlapping ends of cording. Matching wrong sides, glue ornament front and back together.

Needlework adaptation by Nancy Dockter.

Fig. 1

pretty sampling

#1 (41w x 51h)

#2 (37w x 47h)

#3 (41w x 56h)

X	DMC	B'ST
⬚	blanc	
◼	221	/
✕	223	
★	501	/
+	502	
=	503	
▢	610	/
☆	729	/
◼	838	/
◖	924	
◇	927	
△	3721	
⊠	3768	/
○	3774	
•	221	French Knot
•	223	French Knot

Petite Samplers (shown on page 29): Designs #1, #2, and #3 were each stitched over 2 fabric threads on a 7" x 8" piece of Tea-Dyed Irish Linen (36 ct). Two strands of floss were used for Cross Stitch and 1 strand for Backstitch and French Knots. Referring to photo and chart, personalize Designs #1 and #3 using alphabet and numeral provided. They were custom framed.

Designs by Deborah Payne Baker.

VICTORIAN ANGELS

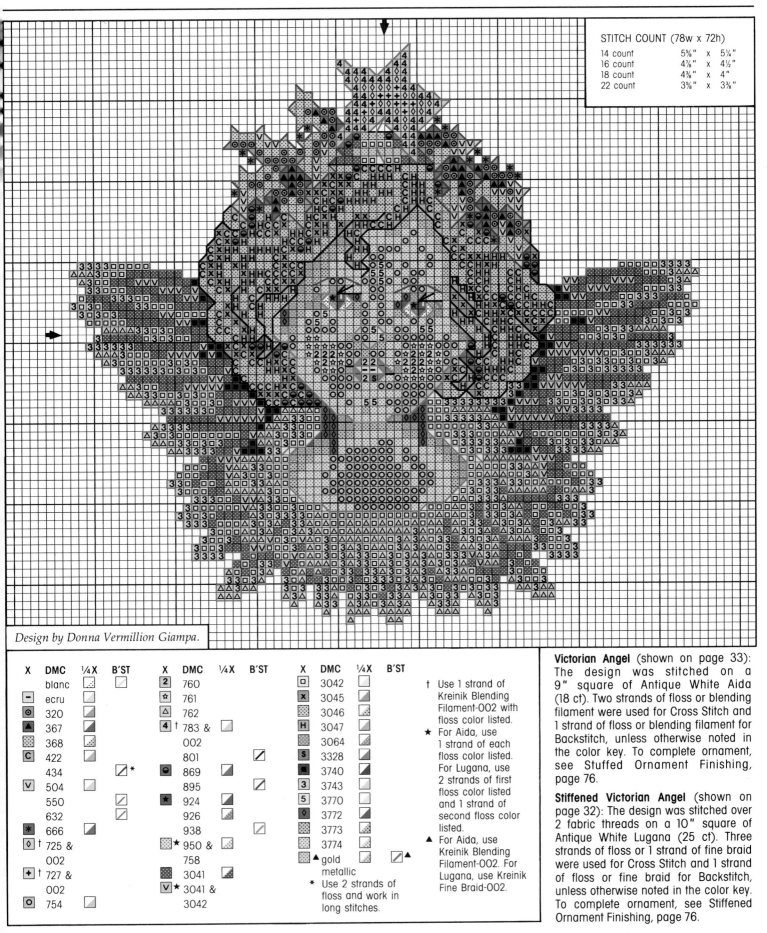

STITCH COUNT (78w x 72h)		
14 count	5⅝"	x 5¼"
16 count	4⅞"	x 4½"
18 count	4⅜"	x 4"
22 count	3⅝"	x 3⅜"

Design by Donna Vermillion Giampa.

X	DMC	¼X	B'ST	X	DMC	¼X	B'ST	X	DMC	¼X	B'ST
	blanc			2	760			□	3042		
-	ecru			☆	761			x	3045		
⊙	320			△	762				3046		
▲	367			4 †	783 &			H	3047		
	368				002				3064		
C	422				801			S	3328		
	434		*	◕	869			■	3740		
V	504				895			3	3743		
	550			★	924			5	3770		
	632				926			◇	3772		
✱	666				938				3773		
◊ †	725 &				950 &				3774		
	002				758			▲	gold		▲
+ †	727 &				3041				metallic		
	002			V ★	3041 &						
○	754				3042						

† Use 1 strand of Kreinik Blending Filament-002 with floss color listed.

★ For Aida, use 1 strand of each floss color listed. For Lugana, use 2 strands of first floss color listed and 1 strand of second floss color listed.

▲ For Aida, use Kreinik Blending Filament-002. For Lugana, use Kreinik Fine Braid-002.

* Use 2 strands of floss and work in long stitches.

Victorian Angel (shown on page 33): The design was stitched on a 9" square of Antique White Aida (18 ct). Two strands of floss or blending filament were used for Cross Stitch and 1 strand of floss or blending filament for Backstitch, unless otherwise noted in the color key. To complete ornament, see Stuffed Ornament Finishing, page 76.

Stiffened Victorian Angel (shown on page 32): The design was stitched over 2 fabric threads on a 10" square of Antique White Lugana (25 ct). Three strands of floss or 1 strand of fine braid were used for Cross Stitch and 1 strand of floss or fine braid for Backstitch, unless otherwise noted in the color key. To complete ornament, see Stiffened Ornament Finishing, page 76.

VICTORIAN ANGELS

Victorian Angels (shown on page 33): Designs #1 and #2 were each stitched on a 9" square of Antique White Aida (18 ct). Two strands of floss or blending filament were used for Cross Stitch and 1 strand of floss or blending filament for Backstitch, unless otherwise noted in the color key. They were made into stuffed ornaments.

STUFFED ORNAMENT FINISHING

For each ornament, you will need a 9" square of Antique White Aida for backing, 6" length of ⅛"w ribbon for hanger, and polyester fiberfill.

Matching right sides and raw edges, pin stitched piece and backing fabric together. Leaving an opening for turning and stuffing, sew backing fabric to stitched piece close to edge of design. Trim seam allowance to ¼" and clip curves; turn right side out. Stuff ornament with polyester fiberfill and blind stitch opening closed.

Match short edges and fold ribbon in half; referring to photo, tack ends to back of ornament.

STIFFENED ORNAMENT FINISHING

(Shown on page 32, chart on page 75) For ornament, you will need a 10" square of lightweight white fabric for backing, fabric stiffener, small foam brush, and angel hair.

Apply a heavy coat of fabric stiffener to back of stitched piece using small foam brush. Matching wrong sides, place stitched piece on backing fabric, smoothing stitched piece while pressing fabric pieces together; allow to dry. Apply fabric stiffener to backing fabric; allow to dry. Cut out close to edge of stitched design. Referring to photo, arrange stiffened design in angel hair.

Designs by Donna Vermillion Giampa.

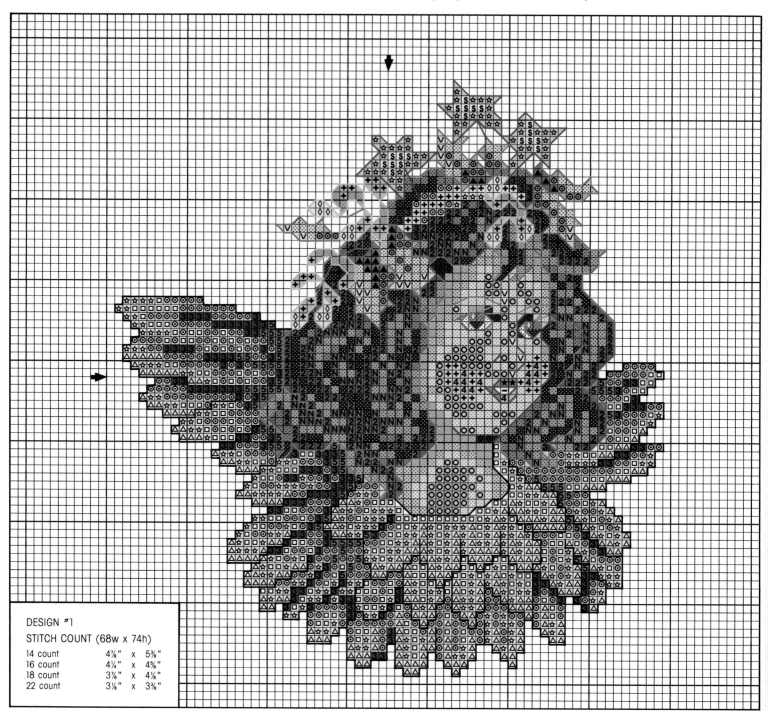

DESIGN #1
STITCH COUNT (68w x 74h)

14 count	4⅞"	x 5⅜"
16 count	4¼"	x 4⅝"
18 count	3⅞"	x 4⅛"
22 count	3⅛"	x 3⅜"

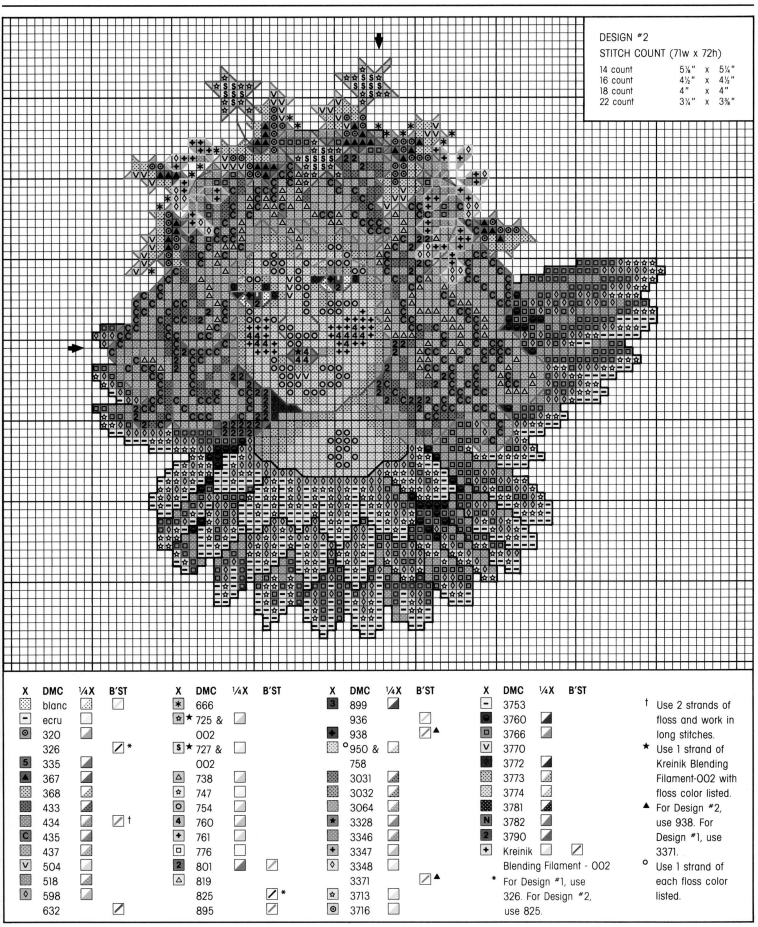

DESIGN #2
STITCH COUNT (71w x 72h)

14 count	5⅛"	x	5¼"
16 count	4½"	x	4½"
18 count	4"	x	4"
22 count	3¼"	x	3⅜"

X	DMC	¼X	B'ST		X	DMC	¼X	B'ST		X	DMC	¼X	B'ST		X	DMC	¼X	B'ST
	blanc				✱	666				▓	899				-	3753		
-	ecru				☆★	725 &					936				◉	3760		
◉	320					002				✦	938		▲		▢	3766		
	326		✱		S★	727 &				▨	°950 &				V	3770		
5	335					002					758				▊	3772		
▲	367				△	738					3031				▓	3773		
▨	368				☆	747					3032					3774		
▓	433				◯	754					3064				▨	3781		
	434		t		4	760				★	3328				N	3782		
C	435				✚	761				✦	3346				2	3790		
	437				▢	776				✚	3347				✦	Kreinik		
V	504				2	801				◇	3348					Blending Filament - 002
	518				△	819					3371		▲			
◇	598					825		✱		☆	3713					
	632					895				◉	3716					

† Use 2 strands of floss and work in long stitches.

★ Use 1 strand of Kreinik Blending Filament-002 with floss color listed.

▲ For Design #2, use 938. For Design #1, use 3371.

° Use 1 strand of each floss color listed.

* For Design #1, use 326. For Design #2, use 825.

77

FROSTY FRIENDS

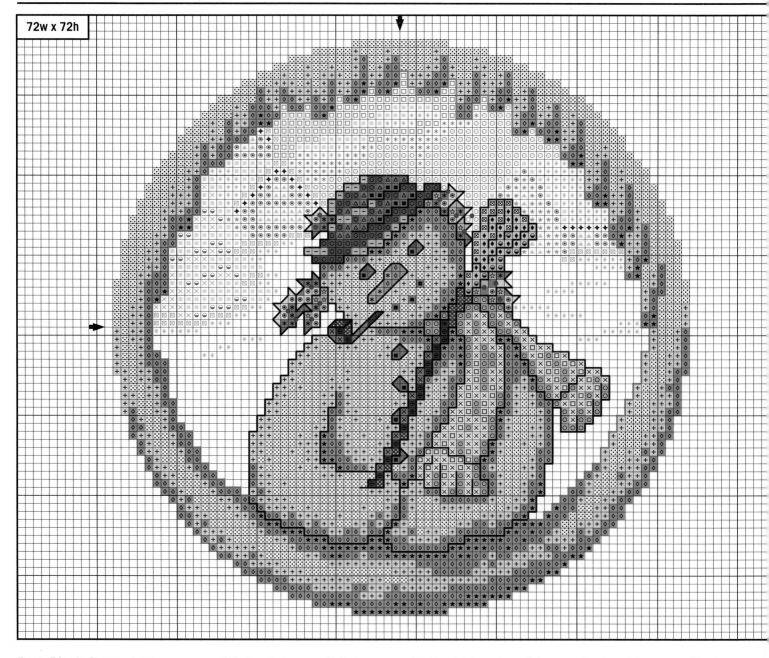

72w x 72h

Frosty Friends Ornament (shown on page 34): The design was stitched over 2 fabric threads on a 9" square of Antique White Belfast Linen (32 ct). Two strands of floss were used for Cross Stitch and 1 strand for Half Cross Stitch, Backstitch, and French Knots.

For ornament, you will need a 6½" dia. circle of Antique White Belfast Linen for backing, two 4½" dia. circles of adhesive mounting board, two 4½" dia. circles of batting, 2" x 17½" bias fabric strip for cording, 17½" length of ¼" dia. purchased cord, 6" length of ¼"w ribbon for hanger, 10" length of ¼"w ribbon for bow, and clear-drying craft glue.

Centering design, trim stitched piece to a 6½" dia. circle.

Remove paper from one piece of mounting board and press one batting piece onto mounting board. Repeat with remaining mounting board and batting.

Clip ½" into edge of stitched piece at ½" intervals. Center wrong side of stitched piece over batting on one mounting board piece; fold edges of stitched piece to back of mounting board and glue in place. Repeat with

backing fabric and remaining mounting board for ornament back.

For cording, center cord on wrong side of bias strip; matching long edge, fold strip over cord. Use a zipper foot to baste along length of strip close to cord; trim seam allowance to ½". Starting at bottom center of stitched piece and 2" from beginning of cording, glue cording seam allowance to wrong side of ornament front; stop 3" from overlapping end of cording. Ends of cording should overlap approximately 2". On overlapping end of cording, remove 2½" of basting; fold end of bias strip back and trim cord so that it meets beginning end of cord. Fold end of bias strip ½" to wrong side; wrap bias strip over beginning end of cording. Finish gluing cording to stitched piece. For hanger, match short ends and fold 6" length of ribbon in half; referring to photo, glue ends to wrong side of ornament front. Matching wrong sides, glue ornament front and back together. Tie 10" length of ribbon in a bow and glue bow to ornament; trim ends as desired.

Needlework adaptation by Nancy Dockter.

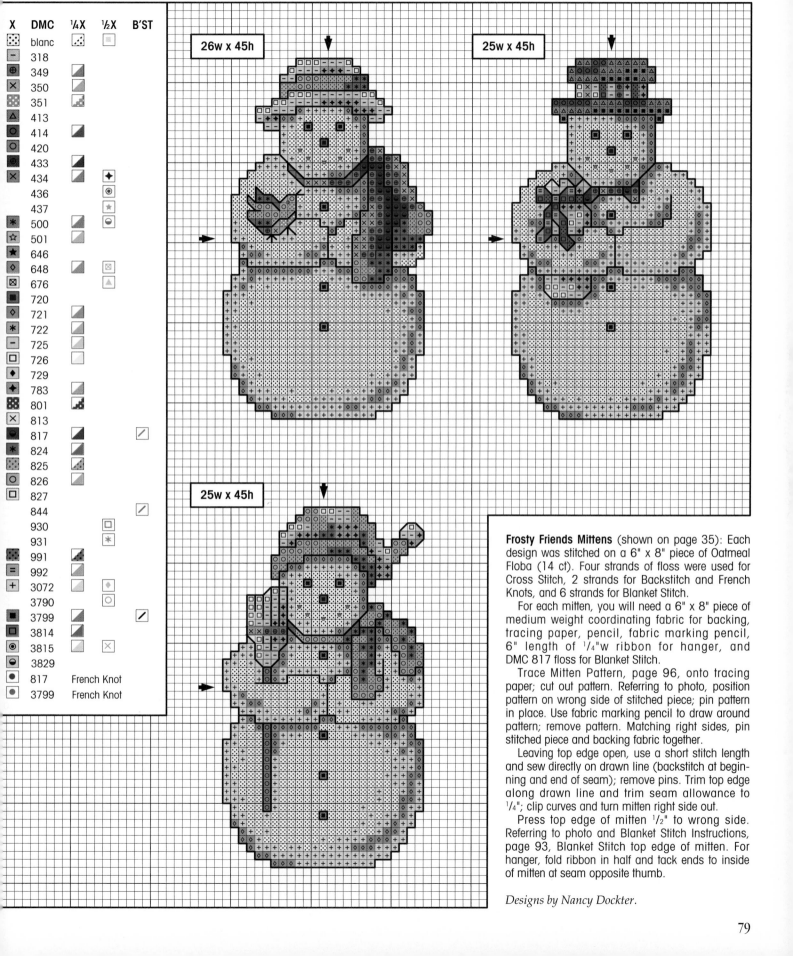

X	DMC	¼X	½X	B'ST
⊠	blanc	⋰	▩	
−	318			
⊕	349	◢		
✕	350	◢		
⊠	351	◢		
△	413			
○	414	◢		
◎	420			
⊞	433	◢		
✕	434	◢	◆	
	436		◉	
	437		★	
✳	500	◢	◒	
☆	501	◢		
★	646			
◇	648	◢	⊠	
⊠	676		▲	
■	720			
◇	721	◢		
✳	722	◢		
−	725			
□	726			
◆	729			
✦	783	◢		
▩	801	◢		
✕	813			
▨	817	◢		╱
✳	824	◢		
⊠	825	◢		
○	826	◢		
□	827			╱
	844			╱
	930		□	
	931		✳	
⊠	991	◢		
=	992	◢		
+	3072	◢	◆	
◒	3790		○	
■	3799	◢		╱
▨	3814	◢		
◉	3815	◢	✕	
◒	3829			
●	817	French Knot		
●	3799	French Knot		

26w x 45h

25w x 45h

25w x 45h

Frosty Friends Mittens (shown on page 35): Each design was stitched on a 6" x 8" piece of Oatmeal Floba (14 ct). Four strands of floss were used for Cross Stitch, 2 strands for Backstitch and French Knots, and 6 strands for Blanket Stitch.

For each mitten, you will need a 6" x 8" piece of medium weight coordinating fabric for backing, tracing paper, pencil, fabric marking pencil, 6" length of ¼"w ribbon for hanger, and DMC 817 floss for Blanket Stitch.

Trace Mitten Pattern, page 96, onto tracing paper; cut out pattern. Referring to photo, position pattern on wrong side of stitched piece; pin pattern in place. Use fabric marking pencil to draw around pattern; remove pattern. Matching right sides, pin stitched piece and backing fabric together.

Leaving top edge open, use a short stitch length and sew directly on drawn line (backstitch at beginning and end of seam); remove pins. Trim top edge along drawn line and trim seam allowance to ¼"; clip curves and turn mitten right side out.

Press top edge of mitten ½" to wrong side. Referring to photo and Blanket Stitch Instructions, page 93, Blanket Stitch top edge of mitten. For hanger, fold ribbon in half and tack ends to inside of mitten at seam opposite thumb.

Designs by Nancy Dockter.

RADIANT NATIVITY

55w x 55h

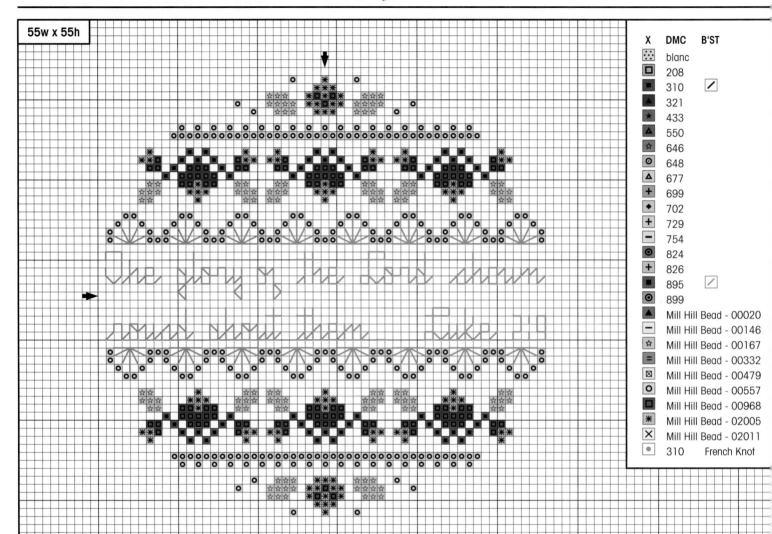

X	DMC	B'ST
⦂⦂	blanc	
▫	208	
■	310	✓
▲	321	
★	433	
△	550	
☆	646	
⊙	648	
△	677	
+	699	
◆	702	
+	729	
−	754	
⊚	824	
+	826	
■	895	✓
⊚	899	
▲	Mill Hill Bead - 00020	
−	Mill Hill Bead - 00146	
☆	Mill Hill Bead - 00167	
=	Mill Hill Bead - 00332	
⊠	Mill Hill Bead - 00479	
⊙	Mill Hill Bead - 00557	
▫	Mill Hill Bead - 00968	
✳	Mill Hill Bead - 02005	
✕	Mill Hill Bead - 02011	
•	310	French Knot

"The Glory of the Lord" Ornament (shown on page 36): The design was stitched on a 5¹/₂" x 8¹/₂" piece of Ivory perforated plastic (14 ct). Three strands of floss were used for Cross Stitch and 2 strands for Backstitch. To attach beads, use 2 strands of DMC 676 floss; see Attaching Beads, page 82.

Centering design, trim perforated plastic to a 4³/₈" dia. circle.

For ornament, you will need a 17" length of ¹/₄" dia. satin cording with attached seam allowance, 17" length of ³/₁₆" dia. gold metallic cording with attached seam allowance, 4⁷/₈" dia. circle of ivory paper, and clear-drying craft glue.

Beginning at center bottom and 1" from end of satin cording, glue seam allowance of satin cording to back of ornament; overlap ends of cording and glue to back of ornament. Beginning at center bottom and 1" from end of gold cording, place gold cording on outside edge of satin cording and glue seam allowance of gold cording to seam allowance of satin cording. Overlap ends of gold cording and glue to back of ornament. Glue paper to back of ornament.

Design by Linda Culp Calhoun.

Nativity Figures (shown on pages 37-39): Each design was stitched on a 5¹/₂" x 8¹/₂" piece of Ivory perforated plastic (14 ct). Three strands of floss were used for Cross Stitch and 1 strand for Backstitch and French Knots. To attach beads, use 2 strands of DMC 676 floss; see Attaching Beads, page 82. Trim perforated plastic close to edges of stitched design.

Designs by Maryanne Moreck.

31w x 30h

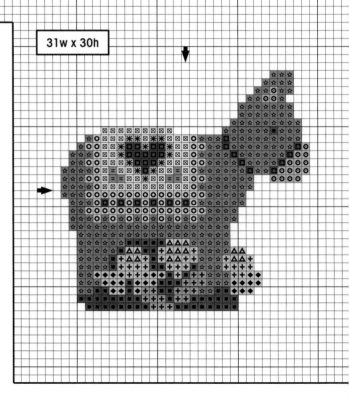

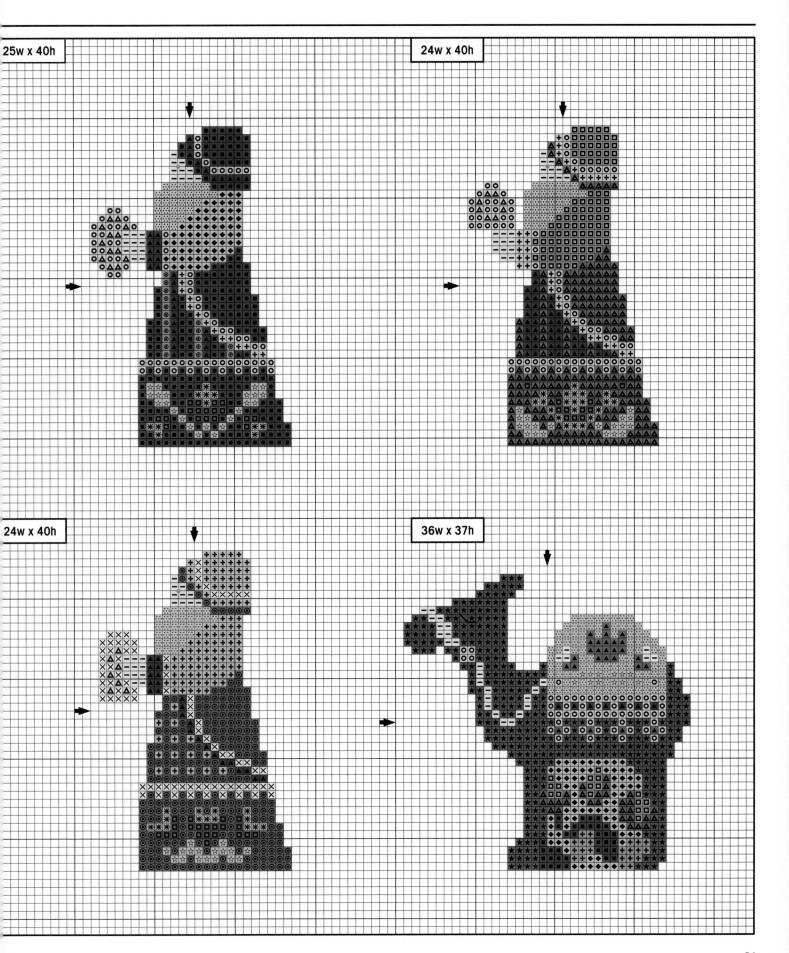

RADIANT NATIVITY

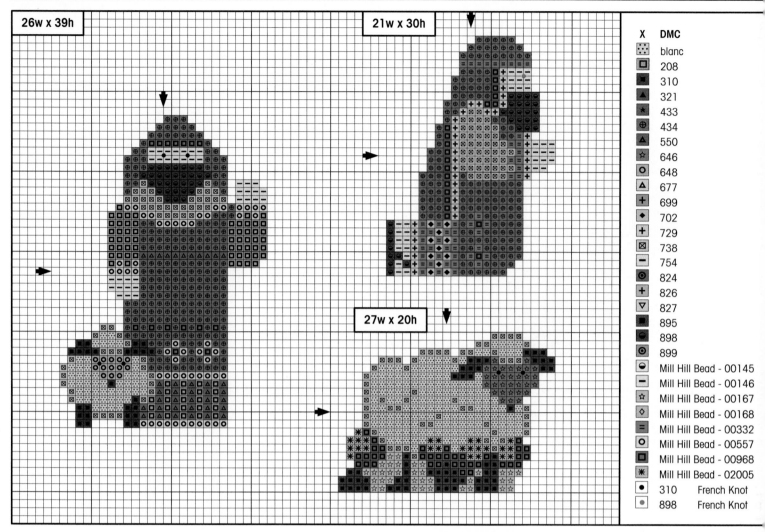

X	DMC	
⋮	blanc	
◻	208	
◼	310	
▲	321	
★	433	
⊕	434	
▲	550	
☆	646	
○	648	
△	677	
+	699	
◆	702	
+	729	
⊠	738	
—	754	
◉	824	
+	826	
▽	827	
■	895	
◕	898	
◉	899	
◔	Mill Hill Bead - 00145	
—	Mill Hill Bead - 00146	
☆	Mill Hill Bead - 00167	
◇	Mill Hill Bead - 00168	
=	Mill Hill Bead - 00332	
○	Mill Hill Bead - 00557	
◻	Mill Hill Bead - 00968	
✳	Mill Hill Bead - 02005	
●	310	French Knot
●	898	French Knot

Nativity Figures (shown on pages 37-39): Each design was stitched on a 5¹⁄₂" x 8¹⁄₂" piece of Ivory perforated plastic (14 ct). Three strands of floss were used for Cross Stitch and 1 strand for French Knots. To attach beads, use 2 strands of DMC 676 floss; see Attaching Beads. Trim perforated plastic close to edges of stitched design.

For each shepherd's staff, you will need an 8" length of #2 round reed, 3 rubber bands, ruler, and wood tone stain. Soak reed in water for 10 minutes, secure reed to ruler using 2 rubber bands; fold reed down 3" from one end and secure with remaining rubber band. Allow to dry completely and remove rubber bands; apply wood stain to reed. Referring to photo, trim ends of reed and glue to shepherd.

Designs by Maryanne Moreck.

Attaching Beads: Referring to chart for bead placement, sew bead in plac using a fine needle that will pass through bead. Bring needle up at 1, ru needle through bead then down at 2 making a Half Cross Stitch (**Fig. 1** Secure floss on back or move to next bead as shown in **Fig. 1**.

Fig. 1

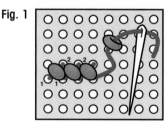

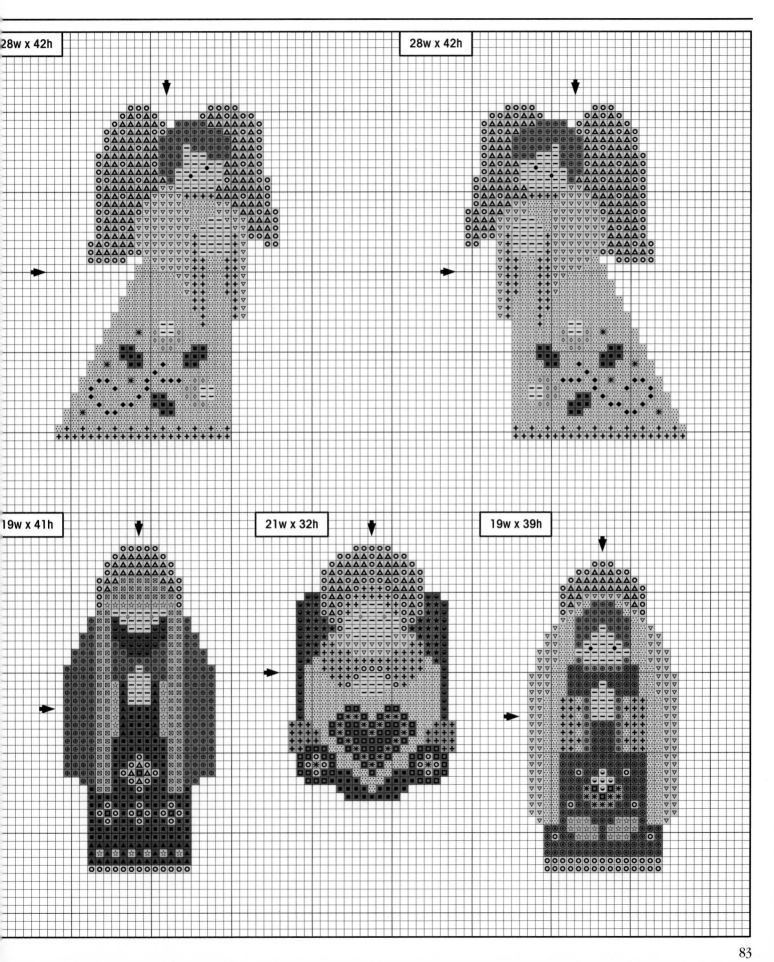

28w x 42h

28w x 42h

19w x 41h

21w x 32h

19w x 39h

MERRY MINI STOCKINGS

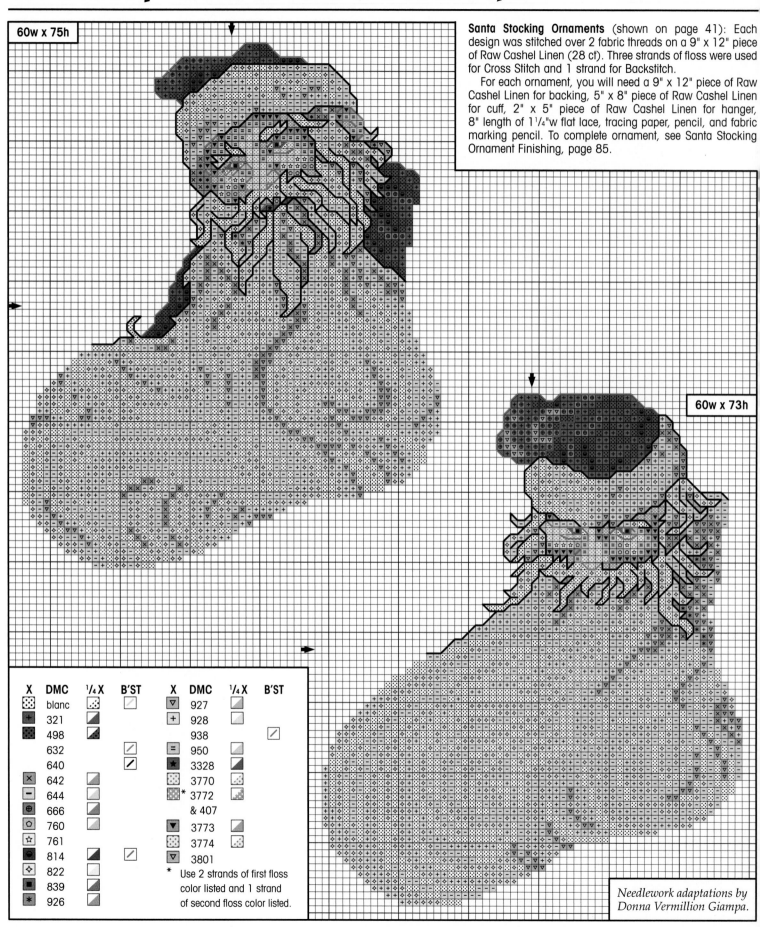

60w x 75h

60w x 73h

Santa Stocking Ornaments (shown on page 41): Each design was stitched over 2 fabric threads on a 9" x 12" piece of Raw Cashel Linen (28 ct). Three strands of floss were used for Cross Stitch and 1 strand for Backstitch.

For each ornament, you will need a 9" x 12" piece of Raw Cashel Linen for backing, 5" x 8" piece of Raw Cashel Linen for cuff, 2" x 5" piece of Raw Cashel Linen for hanger, 8" length of 1¼"w flat lace, tracing paper, pencil, and fabric marking pencil. To complete ornament, see Santa Stocking Ornament Finishing, page 85.

X	DMC	¼ X	B'ST	X	DMC	¼ X	B'ST
	blanc			▽	927		
+	321			+	928		
	498				938		/
	632		/	=	950		
	640		/	★	3328		
×	642				3770		
−	644				3772		
⊕	666				& 407		
⬠	760			▼	3773		
☆	761				3774		
●	814		/	▽	3801		
◇	822						
■	839			* Use 2 strands of first floss			
∗	926			color listed and 1 strand of second floss color listed.			

Needlework adaptations by Donna Vermillion Giampa.

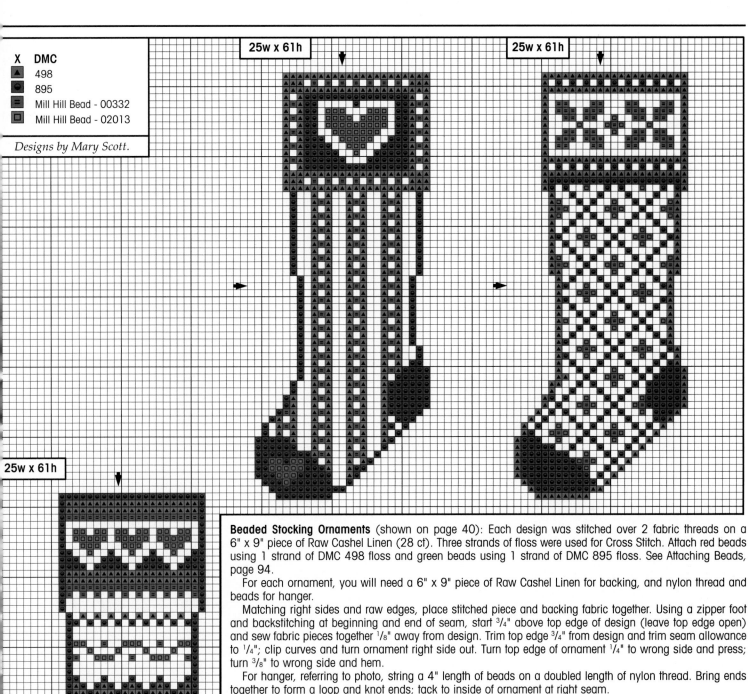

X	DMC	
▲	498	
◉	895	
=	Mill Hill Bead - 00332	
□	Mill Hill Bead - 02013	

Designs by Mary Scott.

25w x 61h

25w x 61h

25w x 61h

Beaded Stocking Ornaments (shown on page 40): Each design was stitched over 2 fabric threads on a 6" x 9" piece of Raw Cashel Linen (28 ct). Three strands of floss were used for Cross Stitch. Attach red beads using 1 strand of DMC 498 floss and green beads using 1 strand of DMC 895 floss. See Attaching Beads, page 94.

For each ornament, you will need a 6" x 9" piece of Raw Cashel Linen for backing, and nylon thread and beads for hanger.

Matching right sides and raw edges, place stitched piece and backing fabric together. Using a zipper foot and backstitching at beginning and end of seam, start ³/₄" above top edge of design (leave top edge open) and sew fabric pieces together ¹/₈" away from design. Trim top edge ³/₄" from design and trim seam allowance to ¹/₄"; clip curves and turn ornament right side out. Turn top edge of ornament ¹/₄" to wrong side and press; turn ³/₈" to wrong side and hem.

For hanger, referring to photo, string a 4" length of beads on a doubled length of nylon thread. Bring ends together to form a loop and knot ends; tack to inside of ornament at right seam.

STOCKING FINISHING

Santa Stocking Ornament Finishing (shown on page 41, charts and supplies on page 84): Trace Santa Stocking Pattern, page 95, onto tracing paper; cut out pattern. Referring to photo, position pattern on wrong side of stitched piece; pin pattern in place. Use fabric marking pencil to draw around pattern; remove pattern. Matching right sides and raw edges, pin stitched piece and backing fabric together.

Leaving top edge open and backstitching at beginning and end of seam, sew directly on drawn line; remove pins. Trim top edge along drawn line. Trim seam allowance to ¹/₄" and clip curves; turn stocking right side out.

Matching right sides and short edges of cuff fabric, use a ¹/₂" seam allowance to sew short edges together. Matching wrong sides and long edges, fold in half and press. Matching raw edges, place cuff inside stocking with cuff seam at center back of stocking. Use a ¹/₂" seam allowance to sew stocking and cuff together; press seam allowance toward cuff. Fold cuff 1¹/₄" over stocking and press. Press short edges of lace ¹/₂" to wrong side. Matching long edges, fold lace in half and press. Beginning and ending at center back, refer to photo and slip lace over cuff and pin in place; on wrong side of cuff, blind stitch lace in place.

For hanger, press each long edge of fabric strip ¹/₂" to wrong side. Matching long edges, fold strip in half; sew close to folded edges. Matching short edges, fold hanger in half and blind stitch to inside of stocking at right seam.

NOAH'S ANIMALS

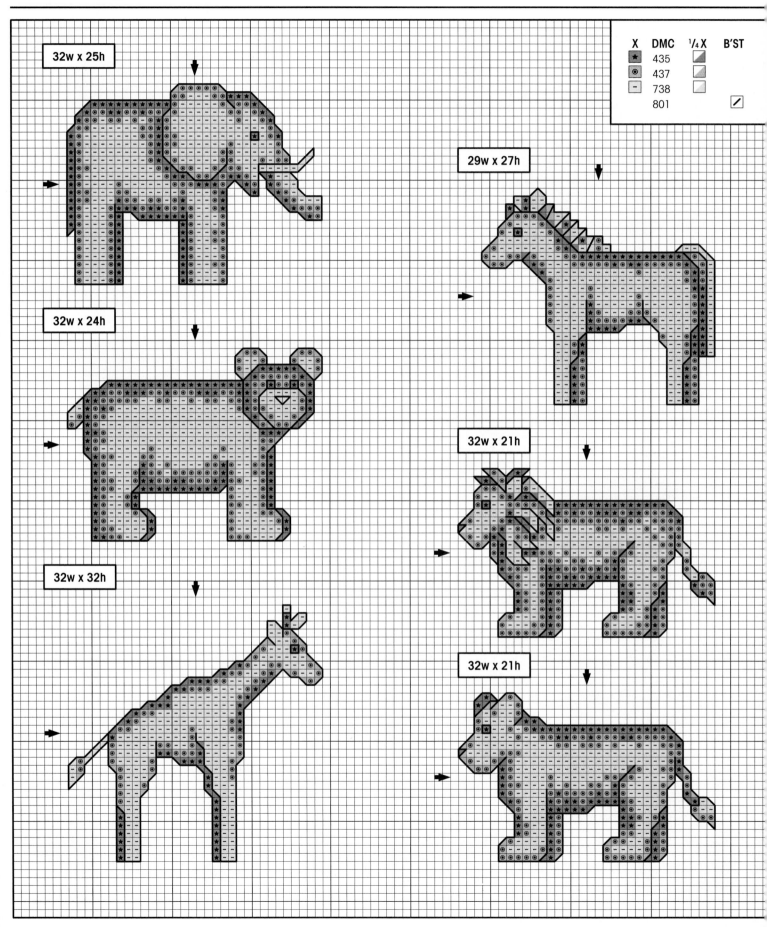

X	DMC	¼X	B'ST
★	435		
◉	437		
−	738		
	801		╱

32w x 25h

29w x 27h

32w x 24h

32w x 21h

32w x 32h

32w x 21h

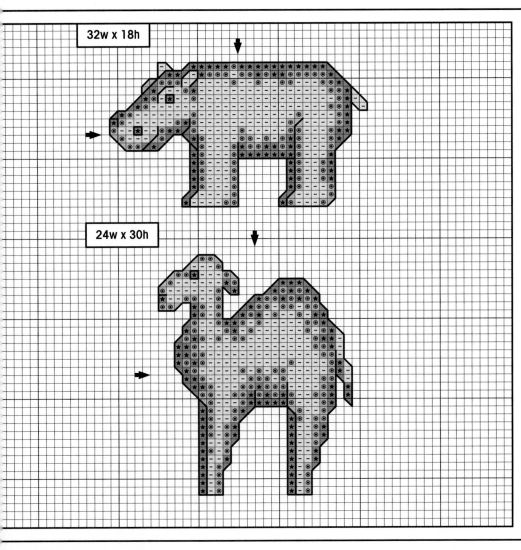

32w x 18h

24w x 30h

Noah's Animals (shown on page 43): Each design was stitched on a 6" square of Ivory Aida (14 ct). Three strands of floss were used for Cross Stitch and 1 strand for Backstitch.

For each animal, you will need a 6" square of lightweight cream fabric for backing, fabric stiffener, small foam brush, poster board, corrugated craft paper, 5" length of $^{1}/_{16}$"w ribbon for hanger, $^{5}/_{8}$" dia. wooden bead, and clear-drying craft glue.

Apply a heavy coat of fabric stiffener to back of stitched piece using small foam brush. Matching wrong sides, place stitched piece on backing fabric, smoothing stitched piece while pressing fabric pieces together; allow to dry. Apply fabric stiffener to backing fabric; allow to dry.

Referring to photo, cut out stiffened piece in a rectangle $^{1}/_{4}$" larger than stitched design on all sides.

Cut poster board in a rectangle slightly smaller than stiffened piece. Center poster board on wrong side of stiffened piece and glue in place.

Cut corrugated craft paper in a rectangle $^{1}/_{4}$" larger on all sides than stiffened piece. Center stiffened piece on corrugated craft paper and glue in place.

For hanger, match short edges and fold ribbon in half; referring to photo, glue ribbon to back of ornament and place wooden bead on hanger.

Designs by Jane Chandler.

FINISHING INSTRUCTIONS

"Good Cheer" Pillow Finishing (shown on page 18, chart on page 62): For pillow, you will need a 5$^{1}/_{2}$" x 5" piece of fabric for backing, 2" x 20" bias fabric strip for cording, 20" length of $^{1}/_{4}$" dia. purchased cord, and polyester fiberfill.

Center cord on wrong side of bias strip; matching long edges, fold strip over cord. Use a zipper foot to baste along length of strip close to cord; trim seam allowance to $^{1}/_{2}$". Matching raw edges, pin cording to right side of stitched piece and make a $^{3}/_{8}$" clip in seam allowance of cording at corners. Ends of cording should overlap approximately 2"; pin overlapping end out of way. Starting 1" from beginning end of cording and ending 2$^{1}/_{2}$" from overlapping end, baste cording to stitched piece. On overlapping end of cording, remove 2" of basting; fold end of fabric back and trim cord so that it meets beginning end of cord. Fold end of fabric $^{1}/_{2}$" to wrong side; wrap fabric over beginning end of cording. Finish basting cording to stitched piece.

Matching right sides and leaving an opening for turning, use a $^{1}/_{2}$" seam allowance to sew stitched piece and backing fabric together. Trim seam allowances to $^{1}/_{4}$" and trim diagonally at corners; turn pillow right side out, carefully pushing corners outward. Stuff pillow with polyester fiberfill and blind stitch opening closed.

Mini Log Carrier Finishing (shown on pages 19-21, charts on page 62): For each carrier, you will need a 12" length of jute twine, 3$^{1}/_{2}$" lengths of twigs (enough for a 1$^{1}/_{4}$" dia. bundle and 2 for handle), and rubber band.

Turn one long edge of stitched piece $^{1}/_{4}$" to wrong side and press; turn $^{1}/_{4}$" to wrong side again and hem. Repeat with remaining long edge. For casing, turn one short edge $^{5}/_{8}$" to wrong side and hem $^{1}/_{2}$" from folded edge. Repeat with remaining short edge.

For handle, insert one twig through one casing of carrier, repeat with another twig and remaining casing. Referring to photo, bring casings together and tie twine around twigs to secure. Gather remaining twigs in a bundle and secure with rubber band; place bundle of twigs in carrier.

Twig-Framed Elf Finishing (shown on pages 19-21, charts on pages 62-63): For each elf, you will need a 7" x 9" piece of lightweight cream fabric for backing, two 7" lengths of twigs, two 5" lengths of twigs, four 6" lengths of jute twine, clear-drying craft glue, fabric stiffener, and small foam brush.

Apply a heavy coat of fabric stiffener to wrong side of stitched piece using small foam brush. Matching wrong sides, place stitched piece on backing fabric, smoothing stitched piece while pressing fabric pieces together; allow to dry. Apply fabric stiffener to backing fabric; allow to dry.

Centering design, trim stiffened piece to measure 3$^{1}/_{2}$" x 5$^{1}/_{2}$". Center one 7" twig on one long edge of stiffened piece and glue in place, repeat with remaining 7" twig and long edge; allow to dry. Center one 5" twig at one short edge of stiffened piece and glue to vertical twigs. Repeat with remaining twig and short edge; allow to dry. Referring to photo, tie one length of jute twine at one corner of stiffened design and trim ends of twine; repeat at each remaining corner.

SANTA'S TOYLAND

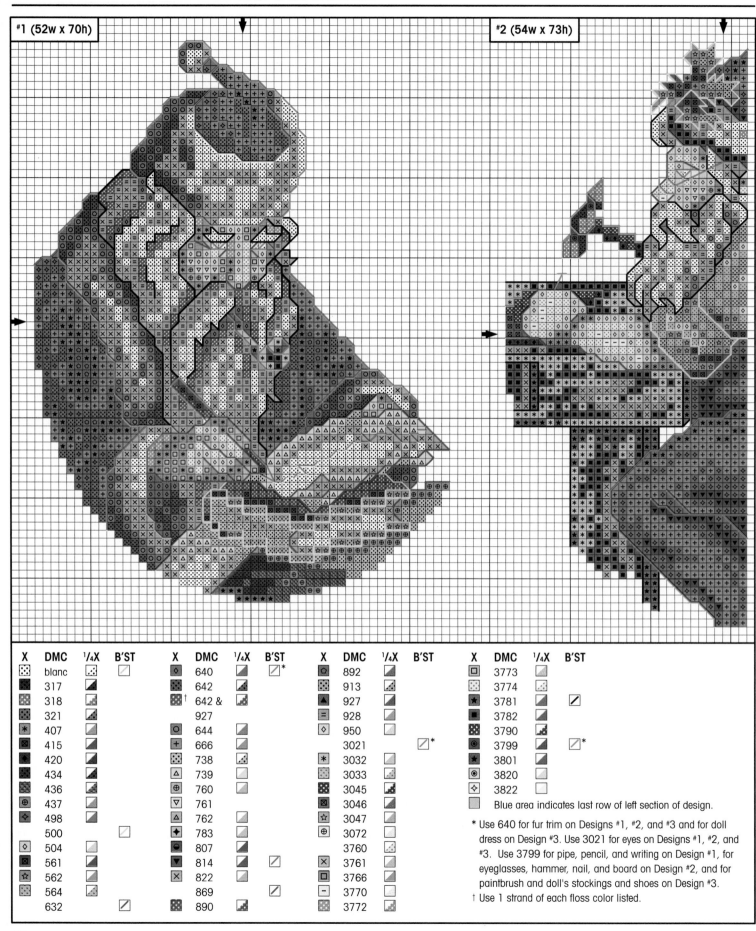

#1 (52w x 70h) #2 (54w x 73h)

X	DMC	¼X	B'ST	X	DMC	¼X	B'ST	X	DMC	¼X	B'ST	X	DMC	¼X	B'ST
	blanc				640		*		892				3773		
	317				642				913				3774		
	318				642 & †				927				3781		
	321				927				928				3782		
	407				644				950				3790		
	415				666				3021		*		3799		*
	420				738				3032				3801		
	434				739				3033				3820		
	436				760				3045				3822		
	437				761				3046						
	498				762				3047						
	500				783				3072						
	504				807				3760						
	561				814				3761						
	562				822				3766						
	564				869				3770						
	632				890				3772						

Blue area indicates last row of left section of design.

* Use 640 for fur trim on Designs #1, #2, and #3 and for doll dress on Design #3. Use 3021 for eyes on Designs #1, #2, and #3. Use 3799 for pipe, pencil, and writing on Design #1, for eyeglasses, hammer, nail, and board on Design #2, and for paintbrush and doll's stockings and shoes on Design #3.

† Use 1 strand of each floss color listed.

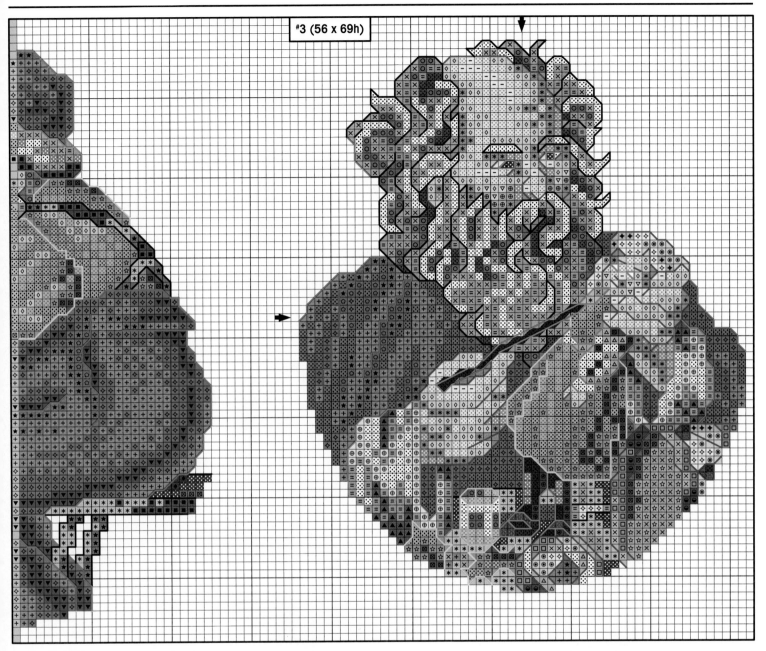

#3 (56 x 69h)

Santa at Work (shown on page 45): Each design was stitched over 2 fabric threads on an 8" square of Tea-Dyed Irish Linen (36 ct). Two strands of floss were used for Cross Stitch and 1 strand for Backstitch.

For each ornament, you will need an 8" square of Tea-Dyed Irish Linen for backing, 10" x 5" piece of adhesive mounting board, tracing paper, pencil, 10" x 5" piece of batting, 2" x 16" bias fabric strip for cording, 16" length of ¼" dia. purchased cord, 6" length of #20 jute twine for hanger, and clear-drying craft glue.

For pattern, fold tracing paper in half and place fold on dashed line of pattern; trace pattern onto tracing paper. Cut out pattern; unfold and press flat. Draw around pattern twice on mounting board and twice on batting; cut out Remove paper from one piece of mounting board and press one batting piece onto mounting board. Repeat with remaining mounting board and batting.

Referring to photo, position pattern on wrong side of stitched piece; pin pattern in place. Cut stitched piece **1" larger** than pattern on all sides. Cut backing fabric same size as stitched piece. Clip ½" into edge of stitched piece at ½" intervals. Center wrong side of stitched piece over batting on

one mounting board piece; fold edges of stitched piece to back of mounting board and glue in place. For ornament back, repeat with backing fabric and remaining mounting board .

For cording, center cord on wrong side of bias strip; matching long edges, fold strip over cord. Use a zipper foot to baste along length of strip close to cord; trim seam allowance to ½". Starting at bottom center of stitched piece and 1½" from beginning of cording, glue cording seam allowance to wrong side of ornament front; stop 3" from overlapping end of cording. Ends of cording should overlap approximately 2". On overlapping end of cording, remove 2½" of basting; fold end of fabric back and trim cord so that it meets beginning end of cord. Fold end of fabric ½" to wrong side; wrap fabric over beginning end of cording. Finish gluing cording to ornament front. For hanger, fold length of jute in half and referring to photo for placement, glue to wrong side of ornament front. Matching wrong sides, glue ornament front and back together.

Needlework adaptations by Donna Vermillion Giampa.

SANTA'S TOYLAND

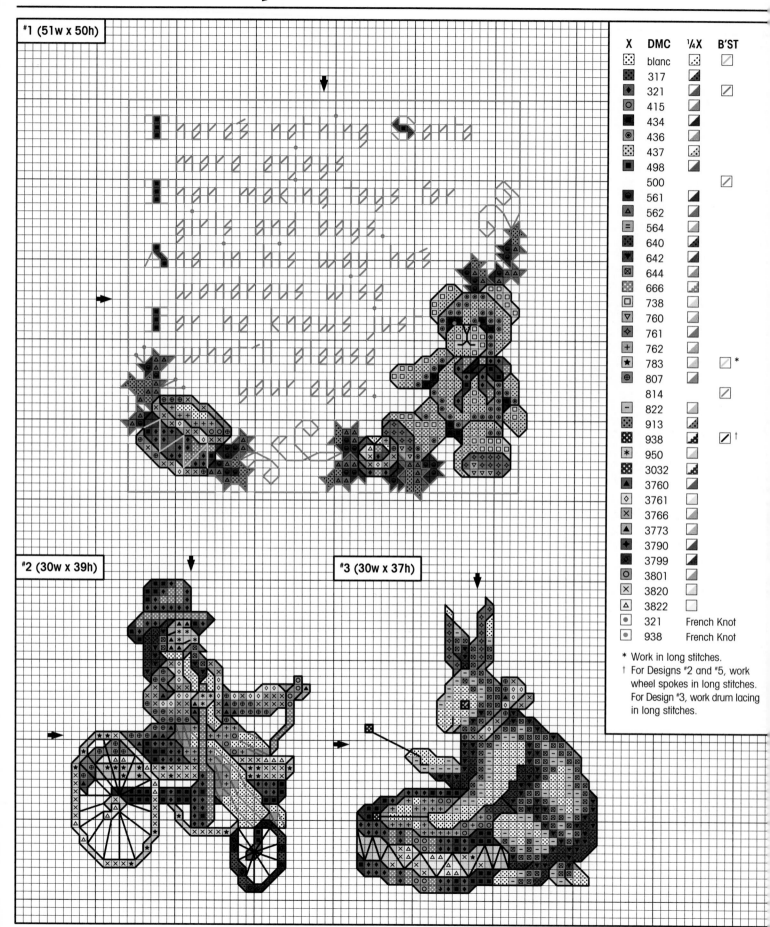

#1 (51w x 50h)

#2 (30w x 39h)

#3 (30w x 37h)

X	DMC	¼X	B'ST
	blanc		
	317		
	321		
	415		
	434		
	436		
	437		
	498		
	500		
	561		
	562		
	564		
	640		
	642		
	644		
	666		
	738		
	760		
	761		
	762		
	783		*
	807		
	814		
	822		
	913		
	938		†
	950		
	3032		
	3760		
	3761		
	3766		
	3773		
	3790		
	3799		
	3801		
	3820		
	3822		
	321	French Knot	
	938	French Knot	

* Work in long stitches.
† For Designs #2 and #5, work wheel spokes in long stitches. For Design #3, work drum lacing in long stitches.

4 (29w x 43h)

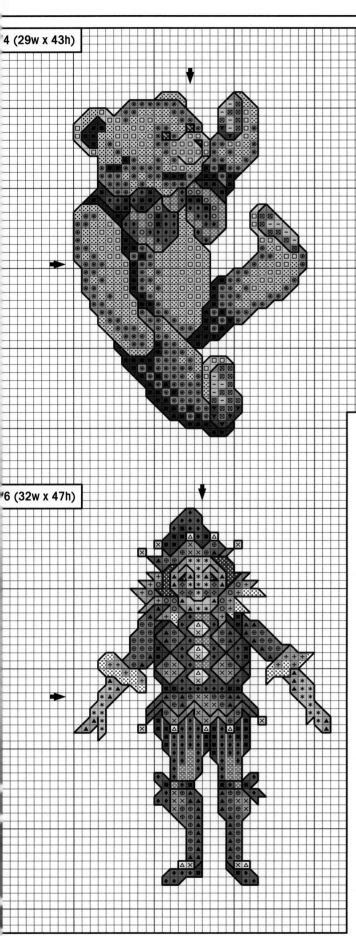

#5 (32w x 38h)

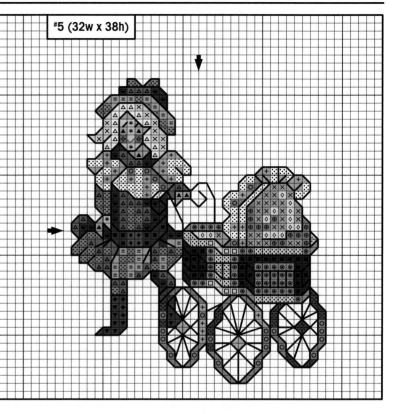

6 (32w x 47h)

Old-time Toys Poem (shown on page 47): Design #1 was stitched over 2 fabric threads on an 8" square of Tea-Dyed Irish Linen (28 ct). Three strands of floss were used for Cross Stitch and 1 strand for Backstitch and French Knots.

For ornament, you will need an 8" square of Tea-Dyed Irish Linen for backing, two 3³/₄" squares of adhesive mounting board, two 3³/₄" squares of batting, 2" x 18" bias fabric strip for cording, 18" length of ¼" dia. purchased cord, 6" length of ¹/₈"w ribbon for hanger, and clear-drying craft glue. To complete ornament, see Old-time Toys Finishing, page 94.

Square Old-time Toys Ornaments (shown on page 46): Designs #2 and #5 were each stitched over 2 fabric threads on a 7" square of Tea-Dyed Irish Linen (28 ct). Three strands of floss were used for Cross Stitch and 1 strand for Backstitch.

For each ornament, you will need a 7" square of Tea-Dyed Irish Linen for backing, two 3¹/₄" squares of adhesive mounting board, two 3¹/₄" squares of batting, 2" x 15" bias fabric strip for cording, 15" length of ¼" dia. purchased cord, 6" length of ¹/₈"w ribbon for hanger, and clear-drying craft glue. To complete ornament, see Old-time Toys Finishing, page 94.

Oval Old-time Toys Ornaments (shown on page 46): Designs #3, #4, and #6 were each stitched over 2 fabric threads on a 7" square of Tea-Dyed Irish Linen (28 ct). Three strands of floss were used for Cross Stitch and 1 strand for Backstitch.

For each ornament, you will need a 7" square of Tea-Dyed Irish Linen for backing, 10" x 5" piece of adhesive mounting board, tracing paper, pencil, 10" x 5" piece of batting, 2" x 14" bias fabric strip for cording, 14" length of ¼" dia. purchased cord, 6" length of ¹/₈"w ribbon for hanger, and clear-drying craft glue.

Trace pattern onto tracing paper; cut out pattern. Draw around pattern twice on mounting board and twice on batting; cut out. Referring to photo, position pattern on wrong side of stitched piece; pin pattern in place. Cut stitched piece **1" larger** than pattern on all sides. Cut backing fabric same size as stitched piece. Clip ½" into edge of stitched piece and backing fabric at ½" intervals. To complete ornament, see Old-time Toys Finishing, page 94.

Designs by Donna Vermillion Giampa.

ENDEARING SNOW BABIES

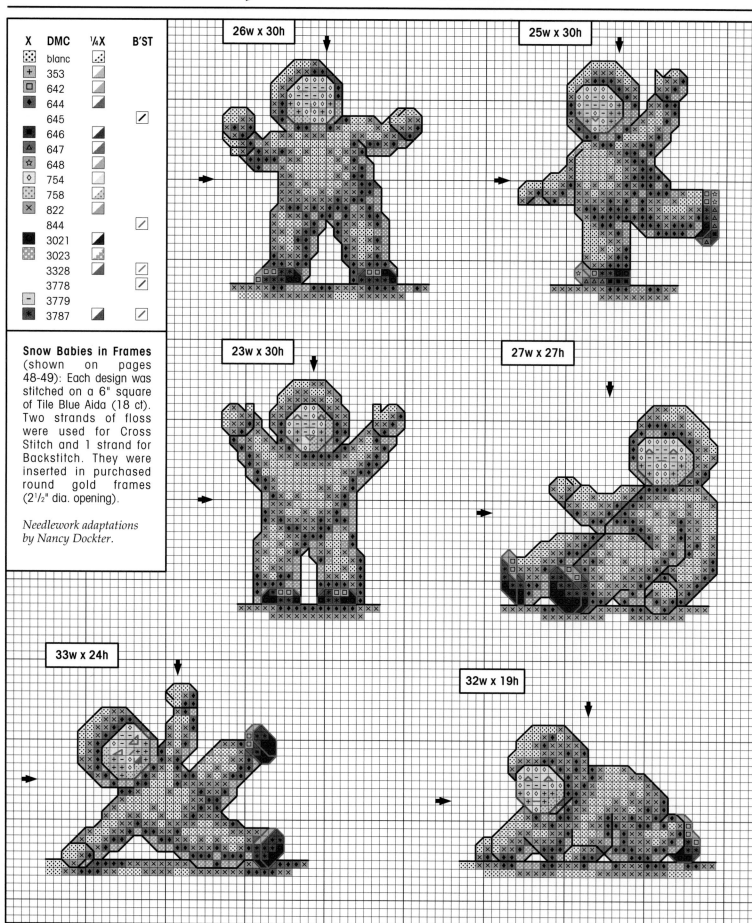

X	DMC	¼X	B'ST
	blanc		
+	353		
□	642		
◆	644		
	645		✓
■	646		
▲	647		
☆	648		
◇	754		
⬙	758		
✕	822		
	844		✓
■	3021		
▦	3023		
	3328		✓
	3778		✓
-	3779		
✳	3787		✓

Snow Babies in Frames (shown on pages 48-49): Each design was stitched on a 6" square of Tile Blue Aida (18 ct). Two strands of floss were used for Cross Stitch and 1 strand for Backstitch. They were inserted in purchased round gold frames (2¹/₂" dia. opening).

Needlework adaptations by Nancy Dockter.

26w x 30h

25w x 30h

23w x 30h

27w x 27h

33w x 24h

32w x 19h

GENERAL INSTRUCTIONS

WORKING WITH CHARTS

How to Read Charts: Each of the designs is shown in chart form. Each colored square on the chart represents one Cross Stitch, one Half Cross Stitch, or a bead placement. Each colored triangle on the chart represents one One-Quarter Stitch or one Three-Quarter Stitch. Black or colored dots represent French Knots or bead placement. The black or colored straight lines on the chart indicate Backstitch. When a French Knot or Backstitch covers a square, the symbol is omitted.

Each chart is accompanied by a color key. This key indicates the color of floss to use for each stitch on the chart. The headings on the color key are for Cross Stitch (**X**), DMC color number (**DMC**), One-Quarter Stitch (**¼X**), Three-Quarter Stitch (**¾X**), Half Cross Stitch (**½X**), and Backstitch (**B'ST**). Color key columns should be read vertically and horizontally to determine type of stitch and floss color. Some designs may include stitches worked with metallic thread such as a Blending Filament, Braid, or Cord. The metallic thread may be blended with floss or used alone. If any of these threads are used in a design, the color key will contain the appropriate information.

Where to Start: The horizontal and vertical centers of each charted design are shown by arrows. You may start at any point on the charted design, but be sure the design will be centered on the fabric. Locate the center of fabric by folding in half, top to bottom and again left to right. On the charted design, count the number of squares (stitches) from the center of the chart to where you wish to start. Then from the fabric's center, find your starting point by counting out the same number of fabric threads (stitches). (**Note:** To work over two fabric threads, count out twice the number of fabric threads.)

How to Determine Finished Size: The finished size of your design will depend on the **thread count per inch** of the fabric being used. To determine the finished size of the design on different fabrics, divide the number of squares (stitches) in the width of the charted design by the thread count of the fabric. For example, a charted design with a width of 80 squares worked on 14 count Aida will yield a design 5¾" wide. Repeat for the number of squares (stitches) in the height of the charted design. (**Note:** To work over two fabric threads, divide the number of squares by one-half the thread count.) Then add the amount of background you want plus a generous amount for finishing. Whipstitch or zigzag the edges of your fabric to prevent raveling.

STITCH DIAGRAMS

Note: Bring threaded needle up at 1 and all odd numbers and down at 2 and all even numbers.

Counted Cross Stitch (X): Work one Cross Stitch to correspond to each colored square on the chart. For horizontal rows, work stitches in two journeys (**Fig. 1**). For vertical rows, complete each stitch as shown (**Fig. 2**). When working over two fabric threads, work Cross Stitch as shown in **Fig. 3**. When the chart shows a Backstitch crossing a colored square (**Fig. 4**), a Cross Stitch should be worked first; then the Backstitch (**Fig. 9 or 10**) should be worked on top of the Cross Stitch.

Fig. 1

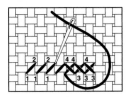

Fig. 2

Fig. 3

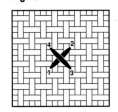

Fig. 4

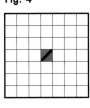

Quarter Stitch (¼X and ¾X): Quarter Stitches are denoted by triangular shapes of color on the chart and on the color key. For a One-Quarter Stitch, come up at 1 (**Fig. 5**); then split fabric thread to go down at 2. When stitches 1-4 are worked in the same color, the resulting stitch is called a Three-Quarter Stitch (¾X). **Fig. 6** shows the technique for Quarter Stitches when working over two fabric threads.

Fig. 5

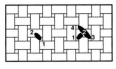

Fig. 6

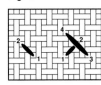

Half Cross Stitch (½X): This stitch is one journey of the Cross Stitch and is worked from lower left to upper right as shown in **Fig. 7**. When working over two fabric threads, work Half Cross Stitch as shown in **Fig. 8**.

Fig. 7

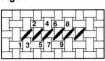

Fig. 8

Backstitch (B'ST): For outline detail, Backstitch (shown on chart and on color key by black or colored straight lines) should be worked after the design has been completed (**Fig. 9**). When working over two fabric threads, work Backstitch as shown in **Fig. 10**.

Fig. 9

Fig. 10

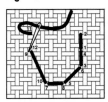

French Knot: Bring needle up at 1. Wrap floss once around needle and insert needle at 2, holding end of floss with non-stitching fingers (**Fig. 11**). Tighten knot; then pull needle through fabric, holding floss until it must be released. For larger knot, use more strands of floss; wrap only once.

Fig. 11

Blanket Stitch: Knot one end of floss. Bring needle up from wrong side at 1, even with edge of fabric. Go down at 2 and come up at 3, keeping floss below point of needle (**Fig. 12**). Continue to stitch in this manner, keeping tension even and stitches evenly spaced (**Fig. 13**).

Fig. 12

Fig. 13

Continued on page 94.

STITCHING TIPS

Working over Two Fabric Threads: Use the sewing method instead of the stab method when working over two fabric threads. To use the sewing method, keep your stitching hand on the right side of the fabric (instead of stabbing the fabric with the needle and taking your stitching hand to the back of the fabric to pick up the needle). With the sewing method, you take the needle down and up with one stroke instead of two. To add support to stitches, it is important that the first Cross Stitch is placed on the fabric with stitch 1-2 beginning and ending where a vertical fabric thread crosses over a horizontal fabric thread (**Fig. 14**). When the first stitch is in the correct position, the entire design will be placed properly, with vertical fabric threads supporting each stitch.

Fig. 14

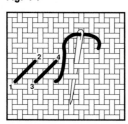

Working on Perforated Paper: Perforated paper has a right side and a wrong side. The right side is smoother and stitching should be done on this side. To find the center, do not fold paper; use a ruler and mark lightly with a pencil or count holes. Perforated paper will tear if handled roughly; therefore, hold the paper flat while stitching and do not use a hoop. Begin and end stitching by running floss under several stitches on back; never tie knots. Use the stab method when stitching and keep stitching tension consistent. Thread pulled too tightly may tear the paper. Carry floss across back as little as possible.

Attaching Beads: Refer to chart for bead placement and sew bead in place using a fine needle that will pass through bead. Bring needle up at 1, run needle through bead then down at 2 making a Half Cross Stitch (**Fig. 15**). Secure floss on back or move to next bead as shown in **Fig. 15**.

Fig. 15

FINISHING INSTRUCTIONS

Young at Heart Stocking Finishing (shown on page 23, chart on page 64): For stocking, you will need a 9" x 12" piece of Tea-Dyed Irish Linen for backing, 1" x 3½" piece of Tea-Dyed Irish Linen for hanger, tracing paper, pencil, and fabric marking pencil.

Trace Young at Heart Stocking Pattern, page 95, onto tracing paper; cut out pattern. Referring to photo, position pattern on wrong side of stitched piece; pin pattern in place. Use fabric marking pencil to draw around pattern; remove pattern. Matching right sides and raw edges, pin stitched piece and backing fabric together.

Leaving top edge open and backstitching at beginning and end of seam, sew directly on drawn line; remove pins. Trim top edge along drawn line; trim seam allowance to ¼" and clip curves. Turn top edge of stocking ¼" to wrong side and press; turn ¾" to wrong side again and hem. Turn stocking right side out.

For hanger, press each long edge of fabric strip ¼" to wrong side. Matching long edges, fold strip in half and sew close to folded edges. Matching short edges, fold hanger in half and blind stitch to inside of stocking at left seam.

Blanket-Stitched Ornament Finishing (shown on pages 24-25, charts and supplies on pages 66-67): Center batting on wrong side of backing fabric. Center wrong side of stitched piece on batting and backing. Pin all layers together. Referring to photo and using an irregular stitch length, Blanket Stitch around ornament through all layers. See Blanket Stitch instructions, page 93.

For "It Won't Be Long" and Tree Ornament hangers, fold lengths of jute in half and tie an overhand knot ½" from ends of jute. Referring to photo, tack jute loops to ornament front; insert stick through loops.

For Stocking and Wreath Ornament hangers, fold length of jute in half and referring to photo, tack ends of jute to ornament back.

Old-time Toys Finishing (shown on pages 46-47, charts and supplies on pages 90-91): Remove paper from one piece of mounting board and press one batting piece onto mounting board. Repeat with remaining mounting board and batting. Center wrong side of stitched piece over batting on one mounting board piece; fold edges of stitched piece to back of mounting board and glue in place. For ornament back, repeat with backing fabric and remaining mounting board.

For cording, center cord on wrong side of bias strip; matching long edges, fold strip over cord. Use a zipper foot to baste along length of strip close to cord; trim seam allowance to ½". Starting at bottom center of stitched piece and 1½" from beginning of cording, glue cording seam allowance to wrong side of ornament front; stop 3" from overlapping end of cording. Ends of cording should overlap approximately 2". On overlapping end of cording, remove 2½" of basting; fold end of fabric back and trim cord so that it meets beginning end of cord. Fold end of fabric ½" to wrong side; wrap fabric over beginning end of cording. Finish gluing cording to stitched piece.

For hanger, match short ends and fold ribbon in half; referring to photo, glue ends to wrong side of ornament front. Matching wrong sides, glue ornament front and back together.

Instructions tested and photo items made by Janet Akins, Lisa Arey, Kandi Ashford, Marsha Besancon, Vicky Bishop, Cecilia Carswell, Alice Crowder, Kathy Elrod, Vanessa Edwards, Jody Fuller, Joyce Graves, Nelwyn Gray, Judy Grim, Muriel Hicks, Joyce Holland, Pat Johnson, Arthur Jungnickel, Melanie Long, Phyllis Lundy, Susan McDonald, Colleen Moline, Jill Morgan, Margaret Moseley, Ray Ellen Odle, Patricia O'Neil, Dave Ann Pennington, Joyce Robinson, Susan Sego, Lavonne Sims, Amy Taylor, Trish Vines, Jane Walker, and Marie Williford.

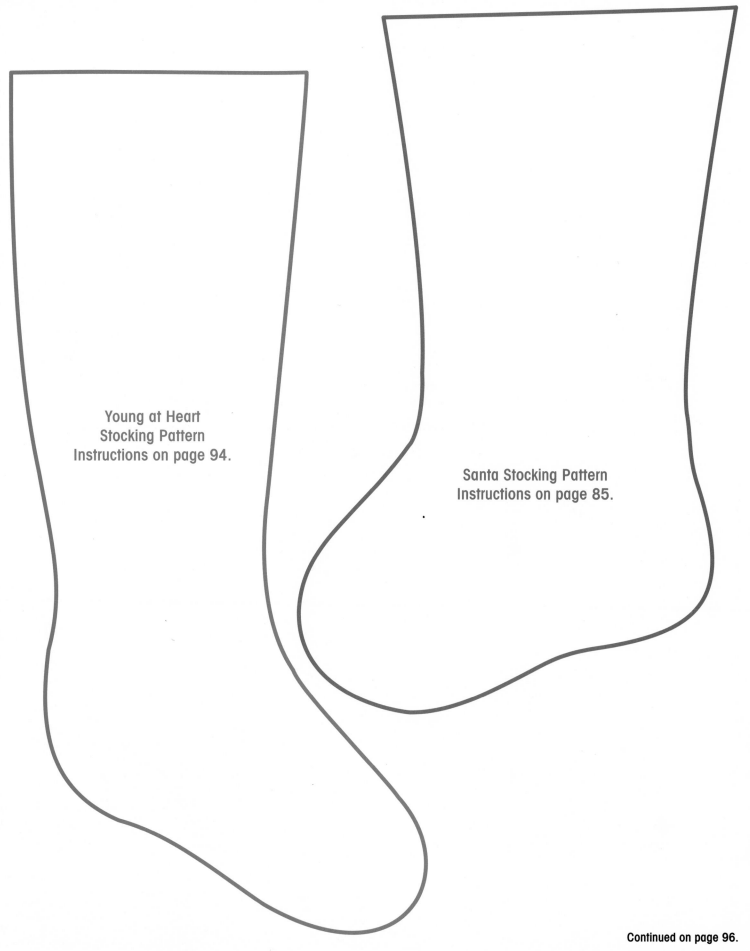

Young at Heart
Stocking Pattern
Instructions on page 94.

Santa Stocking Pattern
Instructions on page 85.

Continued on page 96.

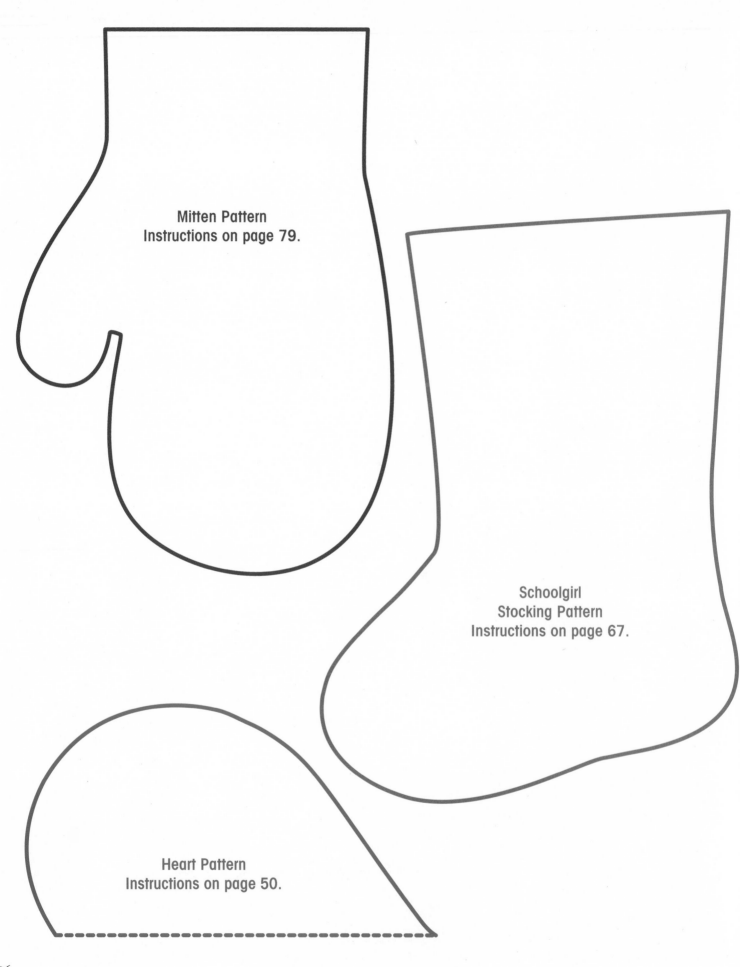

Mitten Pattern
Instructions on page 79.

Schoolgirl
Stocking Pattern
Instructions on page 67.

Heart Pattern
Instructions on page 50.